# GENDERED IMPACTS OF THE COVID-19 PANDEMIC IN CENTRAL AND WEST ASIA

## LESSONS LEARNED AND OPPORTUNITIES FOR GENDER-RESPONSIVE PUBLIC INVESTMENTS

DECEMBER 2023

ASIAN DEVELOPMENT BANK

ADB

Corrigenda to ADB publications may be found at http://www.adb.org/publications/corrigenda.

Note:
In this publication, "$" refers to United States dollars.
ADB recognizes "Kyrgyzstan" as the Kyrgyz Republic.

Cover design by Michael Cortes.

On the cover: ADB has implemented gender-responsive projects in Central and West Asia to support the pandemic response initiatives of developing member countries (ADB photo library).

# Contents

# Tables, Figures, and Boxes

# Abbreviations

| | |
|---|---|
| ADB | Asian Development Bank |
| APVAX | Asia Pacific Vaccine Access Facility |
| COVID-19 | coronavirus disease |
| CPRO | COVID-19 Pandemic Response Action |
| CSO | civil society organization |
| CWA | Central and West Asia |
| DMCs | developing member countries |
| EAG | emergency assistance grant |
| EAL | emergency assistance loan |
| EGM | effective gender mainstreaming |
| GAP | gender action plan |
| GDP | gross domestic product |
| GMM | gender monitoring matrix |
| ILO | International Labour Organization |
| LGBTQI | lesbian, gay, bisexual, transgender, queer or questioning, and intersex |
| MSMEs | micro, small, and medium-sized enterprises |
| SAG | special assistance grant |
| SMEs | small and medium-sized enterprises |
| UCW | unpaid care work |
| UN | United Nations |
| UNICEF | United Nations Children's Fund |
| UNDP | United Nations Development Programme |
| UNFPA | United Nations Population Fund |
| VAWG | violence against women and girls |
| WHO | World Health Organization |

# Executive Summary

Women disproportionately carry the weight of global economic crises. Austerity measures put in place during the economic crises of the 1980s, 1990s, and in 2008 especially affected poor women. The gendered effects of these crises primarily relate to women's roles as unpaid domestic and community care workers, the labor sectors where they work, and their higher labor precarity. It is predicted that the economic crisis triggered by the coronavirus disease (COVID-19) pandemic will be worse than previous crises, impacting women even more.

This study aims to shed light on the extent of the impact of the pandemic, highlighting initiatives and emerging results from policy and public investments, particularly Asian Development Bank (ADB) projects in 9 of the 10 countries in Central and West Asia (CWA): Afghanistan, Armenia, Azerbaijan, Georgia, Kazakhstan, Kyrgyz Republic, Pakistan, Tajikistan, and Uzbekistan.[1] Gendered data on COVID-19 cases and deaths are neither widely available nor updated in all countries across the region. Available data show that in most countries, men were at a higher risk of dying from COVID-19 infection. Some challenges women faced because of the pandemic are negative employment and livelihood impacts in specific sectors, bankrupted women-owned micro, small, and medium-sized enterprises, scarcity of income-generating opportunities, increased burden of unpaid work, overall increase in violence against women and girls (VAWG), and declining mental health. Indirect health effects of the pandemic have been harder to assess given the large data gaps, globally and in CWA. There have certainly been gender-related differences in exposure, as most of the health workforce in the region is female; access to health care, including maternal health, was also disrupted, especially at the beginning of the pandemic.

The response of governments to these gender-related challenges has not been encouraging. Governments face difficulties in developing an inclusive policymaking process in an emergency setting and lack reliable gender data to develop gender-responsive, evidence-based policies and public investment plans. The COVID-19 Global Gender Response Tracker developed by the United Nations Development Programme (UNDP) shows that only about a third of the 232 policy measures implemented by governments in the region in response to COVID-19 were gender sensitive. Over 80% of policy measures that regulate the labor market and social protection were not gender sensitive. In most CWA countries, national legislation exists to promote gender equality and nondiscrimination. However, national statistics and global gender indicators point to persistent gender-based disparities across all countries.

ADB responded quickly and effectively to the pandemic and committed operations at an unprecedented scale. Its support to the COVID-19 response of governments was mainly channeled through the COVID-19 Pandemic Response Option (CPRO), emergency assistance loans, emergency assistance

---

[1]  Turkmenistan declined to participate in the study. ADB placed its regular assistance to Afghanistan on hold effective 15 August 2021.

grants, and special assistance grants, which mostly started in 2020. Projects in the framework of the Asia Pacific Vaccine Access Facility initiative began in 2021. The comprehensive and diverse package of loans and grants, amounting to around $3.64 billion, supported governments in containing and tackling COVID-19 pandemic impacts.

Emerging evidence shows that ADB's efforts to mainstream gender and development considerations into its COVID-19 support have been successful. The inclusion of an effective, pro-poor countercyclical expenditure program as access criteria for CPRO support increased the focus of COVID-19 response operations on social assistance, economic stimulus, and health measures. This expanded financing for social protection and vulnerable groups, including women and girls. The requirement to assess the criteria, together with the gender monitoring matrixes for programs rated as effective gender mainstreaming, enabled ADB to engage in meaningful dialogue with governments on the design and implementation of their COVID-19 response packages with emphasis placed on poor and disadvantaged groups, including women and girls.

For this study, identifying and making recommendations on policy options and priority actions were based on stakeholder interviews and existing (secondary) evidence. Recommendations to improve gender mainstreaming in selected priority areas were developed focusing on ways to (i) increase women's economic security, (ii) prevent and respond to VAWG, (iii) redistribute and regulate unpaid care work, and (iv) improve gender-responsiveness of decision-making in CWA. Both impacts and recommendations are listed in the following table.

## COVID-19 Impacts and Recommendations

| Priority Areas | Impacts |
|---|---|
| **Livelihoods and work, including entrepreneurship and migration** | The pandemic disproportionately impacted women's employment, in terms of job losses, due to (i) the higher vulnerability of women's jobs to external shocks and crises compared to men's, (ii) the structure of labor markets that conform to social norms which restrict women's opportunities, and (iii) the sectors where women's work is culturally acceptable being those hardest hit by the pandemic. |
| | Women-owned businesses, especially micro and small enterprises, are in sectors hardest hit by the pandemic so were disproportionately affected compared to men's. |
| | Decline in remittances of migrant workers especially impacted households left behind in their home countries, where women must resort to other, sometimes unsafe coping strategies, such as taking on additional unprotected work, to provide for their families. |
| **Violence against women and girls** | Stakeholders in CWA countries and across all sectors have identified increases in incidents of VAWG as a consequence of lockdowns and suspension of services. |
| | Conditions associated with pandemic response measures, including isolation, social distancing, and restrictions on movement, together with risk factors like economic stressors and low social support exacerbate VAWG, especially in communities where prevalent social and cultural norms trivialize VAWG. |

*continued on next page*

Table *continued*

| Priority Areas | Impacts |
|---|---|
| Indirect health impacts | Pandemic-induced disruptions in routine health care services, especially in countries with weaker health systems, threaten global progress toward reducing maternal and child morbidity and mortality; sexual and reproductive health care delivery was disrupted; and anecdotal evidence suggests increased depression and anxiety among women. |
| | Majority of health workforces are female, and and have higher exposures to COVID-19; women tend to be more anxious about food insecurity and many coping strategies lead to their undernutrition. |
| | Publicly available gender-disaggregated data on different aspects of women's health and well-being are still incomplete, particularly in Asian countries, so assessing impact is challenging. |
| Unpaid care and domestic work | Lockdowns and restrictions to mobility revealed that, in most households, women are still disproportionately in charge of care and domestic work. Closure of schools and childcare facilities placed additional burdens on women, whose responsibilities in caring for children and family members, including sick family members, increased. |
| | The pandemic has highlighted that the interventions of development organizations have not really penetrated the domestic space as they have not addressed the unequal division of unpaid care and domestic work between women and men. |
| Decision-making and public finance management | Gendered impacts of the pandemic on decision-making and public finance management are still to be fully understood, given the specific and varying timelines of political and electoral processes in the region. |
| | Task forces created in response to the pandemic indicate that appropriate representation or diversity in crisis management has yet to be achieved. |
| | The pandemic also shed light on existing imbalances in regard to policymaking processes, which lack inclusiveness and are not sufficiently consultative. |
| | Limited gender data availability as a crosscutting issue was also identified as a priority problem by many key stakeholders across CWA; it particularly affects decision-making, limiting the possibility of developing evidence-based effective policy. |
| Intersecting vulnerabilities | Women who are informal, unpaid workers or heads of migrant households were particularly vulnerable to economic shocks. Women from ethnic minorities and displaced communities also faced increased risks in crisis situations across the subregion. |
| | Vulnerability of rural women, ethnic minorities, displaced people, and persons with disabilities was exacerbated by the pandemic as evidenced by their lack of access to health care and increased exposure to VAWG. Due to the hardships caused by the pandemic, adolescent and child girls have become even more vulnerable to harmful practices such as child marriage. |
| | LGBTQI communities have also been proven to be especially vulnerable to crisis, with their increased lack of access to economic opportunities and adequate health care, as well as increased risk of violence. |

*continued on next page*

Table *continued*

| Priority Areas | Recommendations |
|---|---|
| **Livelihoods and work, including entrepreneurship and migration** | Strengthen social protection systems and reduce vulnerability of women who are informal or seasonal workers. |
| | Develop regulations that eliminate discriminatory practices toward women in the workplace and ensure a fairer and broader coverage of labor market institutions, including minimum wages and employment protection, as well as improved protection of women from violence and harassment at work. |
| | Reshape skills development in line with post-COVID-19 labor demand, including reducing digital gender gap, and encouraging and supporting women's and girls' education and training in new fields and STEM. |
| | In countries where agriculture is one of the main sectors of employment for women, more attention should be paid to women's terms of inclusion in agriculture, addressing the persistently informal character of female agricultural labor and ensuring that women farmers are not left behind in efforts to promote agriculture value chain enterprises. Policies related to land, agricultural extension services, and technology should be designed and implemented in gender-responsive ways. |
| | Labor market policies can regulate that public procurement be used as an incentive to generate employment for women in sectors where they are likely to predominate. Likewise, public work programs can be used to especially support poor women dependent on casual work for survival. |
| | Develop women's entrepreneurship by promoting a broad-based and mutually reinforcing policy infrastructure. Design and implement holistic interventions, combining capacity building, networking, and access to finance components in line with existing global evidence. Identified measures include increasing the degree of gender integration into the finance sector itself and leveraging information and communications technology for women's entrepreneurial development. |
| | Put in place gender-responsive macroeconomic policies to create an environment conducive to women's economic security. |
| **Violence against women and girls** | Improve the systems that prevent and respond to VAWG is called for across the region. Inherent to these systems is to normalize non-acceptance of any form of VAWG. |
| | Review existing legislation for its (in)adequacy in effectively preventing and eliminating VAWG. Where no laws on VAWG exist, such laws urgently need to be passed then implemented. |
| | Improve referral systems and strengthen or establish multisectorial response mechanisms. |
| | Improve and increase the number of shelters and other protections services, has been highlighted in nearly all CWA countries. Provide adequate training for law-enforcement staff and health and social workers, and further develop digital systems that were introduced during the pandemic. Sufficient funding that guarantees longer-term access to effective services for victims and survivors is therefore an absolute necessity. |
| **Indirect health impacts** | Develop or improve crisis preparedness plans, including increasing support to medical staff who respond to crises. |
| | Enhance gender sensitivity of doctors and medical staff through sustained capacity-building programs. |

*continued on next page*

Table *continued*

| Priority Areas | Recommendations |
|---|---|
| | Increase attention to intersecting forms of vulnerability, for example, women with disabilities faced with barriers that prevented them from accessing routine health care services during the pandemic, or poor women's or adolescent girls' lack of access to reproductive health services. |
| **Unpaid care and domestic work** | Recognize and represent UCW in policies and decision-making, which implies carrying out a detailed analysis of the care economy in each country and of the gaps in the public provisioning of care services for various groups. This includes looking in-depth into the availability of services for both preschool and school-age children, older persons, and persons with disabilities. Social protection policies and programs should support unpaid caregivers and avoid penalizing women for this role. |
| | Strengthen employment rights and workplace policies, including by formalizing parental leave for both women and men, as well as improving awareness of the benefits of flexible work schedules and different types of working arrangements that facilitate more equal distribution of UCW. |
| | Invest in and prioritize social care infrastructure, such as accessible and affordable child and elder care public services. Gender-responsive budgeting initiatives at the macroeconomic and local levels can help to ensure that resources are allocated to such public investments. |
| | Develop a new narrative to dispel social norms that justify women's disproportionate burden of unpaid work. |
| **Decision-making and public finance management** | Improve and develop more meaningful cooperation between civil society and governments in policymaking processes. |
| | Improve gender expertise within governments, including developing capacities for gender analysis of laws and policies, using gender statistics, and practicing gender-sensitive public procurement, which can be a useful tool for developing labor policies that value women's work |
| | Develop and pass gender equality laws and programs in CWA countries without them and improve the implementation of institutional and legal frameworks on gender equality in countries where they exist. Improve intra-governmental coordination in the implementation of gender equality laws. |
| | Renew efforts to strengthen gender-responsive budgeting initiatives. |
| | Improve production and use of timely, quality, comparable gender data by all data sources. Gender data with adequate granularity (disaggregated by ethnic group, disability, income groups etc.) is critical to design gender-responsive and evidence-based policies and promote an equitable recovery. |
| | Address methodological issues and develop capacities in research structures and in different layers of the statistical system for good quality data collection, especially in generating VAWG statistics. |
| **Intersecting vulnerabilities** | Consider intersecting vulnerabilities due to living with a disability, migrant status, ethnicity, location, belonging to the LGBTQI community, or other factors in policymaking in priority areas. |

COVID-19 = coronavirus disease; CWA = Central and West Asia; LGBTQI = lesbian, gay, bisexual, transgender, queer or questioning, and intersex; STEM = science, technology, engineering, and mathematics; UCW = unpaid care work; VAWG = violence against women and girls.
Source: Author.

# Chapter 1

# Introduction

Besides the death and disease caused by COVID-19, the pandemic threatens 2 decades of progress in human development. The systemic crisis caused by the pandemic deepened and revealed social inequalities. Disparities related to the capacity and quality of public health systems emerged clearly, as did widely different levels of social and economic vulnerability, across and within communities.

As United Nations (UN) Secretary-General Antonio Guterres highlighted, "the fallout has shown how deeply gender inequality remains embedded in the world's political, social, and economic systems. (...) The damage is incalculable and will resound down the decades into future generations."[2]

The consequences of economic crises fall disproportionately on women, particularly poor women. This happened with austerity measures implemented in Latin America during the 1980s and 1990s, which saw many services transferred from the public to the private sector, as well as with the 2008 crisis in Southeast Asia and sub-Saharan Africa.[3] The gendered effects of these crises were mainly related to women's roles as unpaid workers in the domestic and community care systems, to the labor sectors that they were mainly working in, as well as to their high labor precariousness.

The economic crisis triggered by the COVID-19 pandemic is expected to be much deeper than previous crises, so women will be hit even harder.[4] Observers have expressed concern over the resources required to face the crisis, stressing that many developing countries do not have the same fiscal capacity as high-income countries. There is an additional and tangible risk that in a context of scarce resources, funds initially allocated to initiatives that contribute to women's rights are redirected elsewhere.

It is therefore essential to keep attention focused on the gender divides that are deepening across the globe and especially in developing countries, including in Central and West Asia (CWA). The purpose of this study is to shed light on the impact of the pandemic and highlight operationally relevant initiatives and emerging results of the COVID-19 response in the region, particularly those that concern initiatives and other public investment of the Asian Development Bank (ADB). Findings should contribute to mainstreaming gender in the design and preparation of projects in CWA, particularly

---

[2]    A. Guterres. 2021. UN Secretary-General's Opening Remarks at the 65th Commission on the Status of Women. 18 March.

[3]    L. Beneria. 1999. Structural Adjustment Policies. In J. Peterson and M. Lewis, eds. *The Elgar Companion to Feminist Economics.* Cheltenham, UK, and Northampton, USA: Edward Elgar; and N. Craviotto. 2010. *The Impact of the Global Economic Crisis on Women and Women's Human Rights Across Regions.* Toronto: Association for Women's Rights in Development.

[4]    United Nations Development Programme (UNDP). 2020. *The Economic Impacts of COVID-19 and Gender Equality. Recommendations for Policymakers.* Panama.

post-COVID-19 recovery efforts, while facilitating the development of subprojects for key sectors. Users of the assessment will be ADB and its resident missions, developing member countries, and possibly development partners of CWA countries.

# Chapter 2

# Scope and Methodological Approach

The idea of an assessment of the gendered impacts of COVID-19 in CWA was developed within the framework of ADB's regional technical assistance program, Preparing and Implementing Gender-Inclusive Projects in Central and West Asia, Subproject 2: Preparing and Monitoring Gender Actions and Targets in Central and West Asia Operations.[5] This project provides support to improve the integration of gender in project design and to promote effective implementation, monitoring, and reporting on the progress of gender action plans (GAPs) and gender targets in CWA.

A draft version was presented at a subregional gender workshop organized by ADB in March 2022. Nine out of ten countries comprising CWA were considered in the study: Afghanistan, Armenia, Azerbaijan, Georgia, Kazakhstan, Kyrgyz Republic, Pakistan, Tajikistan, and Uzbekistan (footnote 1).

## Methodological Approach

To develop the study design, a preliminary review of available gender-relevant secondary data, particularly gender assessments of the impact of COVID-19 as well as quantitative data, was carried out. The review found some information on gendered COVID-19 impacts in reports prepared by international organizations such as UN Women, United Nations Development Programme (UNDP), and the Organisation for Economic Co-operation and Development for some countries in CWA.[6] The Center for Global Development had produced and updated reviews of existing evidence on gendered COVID-19 impacts in low- and middle-income countries, focusing broadly on socioeconomic impacts as well as secondary health effects.[7] This preliminary review helped redefine the scope of this study to four areas:

1.  Livelihoods and work, including entrepreneurship and migration;
2.  Unpaid care and domestic work;
3.  Gender-based violence and women's health; and
4.  Decision-making and public finance management.

---

[5] ADB. *Technical Assistance Report: Preparing and Implementing Gender-Inclusive Projects in Central and West Asia. Subproject 2: Preparing and Monitoring Gender Actions and Targets in Central and West Asia Operations.* Manila.

[6] UNDP and United Nations Children's Fund (UNICEF). 2021. *Progress at Risk. Gender Equality in COVID-19 Response in Europe and Central Asia.* Istanbul; and UN Women. 2021. *Assessing the Lights and Shadows of COVID-19: A Gender Analysis of Pandemic-Related Impacts on Women and Girls in Europe and Central Asia.* Istanbul. It should be noted that these regional assessments refer to regions with different compositions than ADB's CWA. For example, UN's Europe and Central Asia region includes Türkiye and parts of Eastern Europe but not Pakistan or Afghanistan.

[7] M. O'Donnell et al. 2021. The Impacts of COVID-19 on Women's Social and Economic Outcomes: An Updated Review of the Evidence. *Centre for Global Development Policy Paper.* No. 225. Washington, DC: Center for Global Development.

The preliminary review of secondary quantitative data also confirmed that up-to-date gender data in the region is quite limited, as is its granularity (i.e., disaggregation by ethnicity, disability, etc.) and international comparability, which evidently poses a challenge to assess impacts regionally.

A mixed methodological approach was used for this assessment, including desk work, descriptive quantitative analysis, and qualitative research techniques (Table 1). Qualitative techniques included desk reviews of national and regional reports, briefs, and articles by international organizations, academia, and research organizations. Qualitative interviews of key stakeholders were also carried out. Available secondary quantitative data were also collected and analyzed at country and subregional levels, considering the limitations.

## Table 1: Methodological Approach

| Source of Data | | Data Analysis Method |
|---|---|---|
| **Primary** | **Secondary** | **Mixed Methods** |
| • **Key Stakeholder Qualitative Survey** | • Quantitative data from global databases (e.g., World Bank indicators, Inter-Parliamentarian Union Open Data) | • Descriptive statistical analysis |
| | • National, regional, and global reports, briefs and articles, by international organizations, academia, and research organizations | • Desk review |
| | • United Nations Development Programme's Global Gender Response Tracker on governments' COVID-19 response measures | • Qualitative analysis |
| | • Asian Development Bank projects database | |

COVID-19 = coronavirus disease.
Source: Author.

Interviews with key stakeholders were carried out in 8 CWA countries and involved 88 informants.[8] These were selected based on their knowledge and roles in the different contexts in which they operate with the help of ADB gender and social development specialists in each CWA country. Informants were intentionally sampled to obtain views of governments, civil society organizations (CSOs), and development partners dealing with women's rights and gender equality in the four priority areas defined earlier.[9] The views of stakeholders on the main challenges posed by the pandemic were collected, as well as specific actions and policies that they consider adequate to address identified priorities. References to reliable data and existing studies were also requested from stakeholders. Interviews were carried out by national research assistants. Survey results were then triangulated with findings from other secondary sources.

---

[8]    Interviews were not carried out in Afghanistan. ADB placed its regular assistance on hold in Afghanistan effective 15 August 2021.
[9]    A table detailing the number of respondents and interviewees per sector is included in the appendix. The names of respondents and interviewees are not identified in the report for confidentiality.

A review of governments' COVID-19 response initiatives in the region was also carried out, with a focus on ADB-funded initiatives.[10] This review aimed to identify emerging evidence on lessons or opportunities to improve gender-responsiveness of public investments in the region. A discussion on different ways of integrating a gender perspective in policymaking and programming is presented in Box 1 and is a useful reference for understanding the rest of this study.

This assessment has some limitations. A general methodological limitation is that the pandemic was an ongoing phenomenon in March 2022 at the time of writing, so any assessment done at this stage is necessarily partial. The limited availability, granularity, and comparability of statistics in countries of the region are also important methodological constraints for impact evaluation. Connected to this, is that gender data production efforts by development partners and governments in 2020 were not matched by similar efforts in 2021, which means that some findings and studies on the COVID-19 impacts are based on data from the initial phase of the pandemic. Moreover, judgmental sampling, i.e., the non-probability sampling used to select key stakeholders for the survey, presents some weaknesses, as what constitutes a representative sample depends highly on the on the choice of the experts.

Finally, while this assessment was being carried out, the pandemic was still widespread, with the fourth wave ongoing in many countries of the region. This posed some challenges to timely data collection.

---

### Box 1: The Gender Continuum in Policymaking and Programming

Approaches used to integrate a gender perspective in policy and programming have evolved in the last decades, with some variety in definitions used by different actors. It is therefore useful to frame analysis following a gender continuum.

At one end of the continuum is gender-blind programming, which ignores gender differences and the differing needs of women, men, boys, and girls, as well as gender power dynamics within communities.

At the other end is the gender-transformative approach, where programming is designed around a fundamental aim of addressing root causes of gender inequality within society and transforming gender relations, following the 2030 Sustainable Development Goal Agenda. This approach has been taken up by Asian Development Bank, which in its 2030 Gender Strategy vowed to go beyond standard gender mainstreaming to integrate Sustainable Development Goal 5's Transformative Gender Agenda into its programming.

Along this continuum lie gender-responsive initiatives that include specific actions to reduce gender inequalities and gender-sensitive programming that (i) recognize the different needs of women, men, boys, and girls; and (ii) acknowledge gender power dynamics, but do not necessarily address these other than to try and integrate an understanding of these dynamics within program design.

Source: United Nations Population Fund and United Nation's Children's Fund. 2021. *Gender Responsive and/or Transformative Approaches*. New York; and ADB. 2019. *Strategy 2030. Operational Plan for Priority 2. Accelerating Progress in Gender Equality, 2019–2024*. Manila.

---

[10]  Information on governments' COVID-19 responses came from UNDP's Global Gender Response Tracker. Data on ADB initiatives were mainly accessed through its public online database.

# Chapter 3

# Direct Effects of COVID-19 in Central and West Asia: Cases, Deaths, and Stringency of Restrictions

As WHO and other observers have highlighted, some countries have probably underreported COVID-19 cases for a range of reasons, including limited testing. Figure 1 should therefore be interpreted with this limitation in mind.

The countries with most cumulated cases as of February 2022 in absolute terms in CWA are Georgia and Pakistan. However, in relative terms, over 40.7% of Georgia's population tested positive to COVID-19 from January 2020 to February 2022, showing one of the highest ratios in the world, followed by Armenia (13.9%), Azerbaijan (7.5%), and Kazakhstan (also 7.4%).

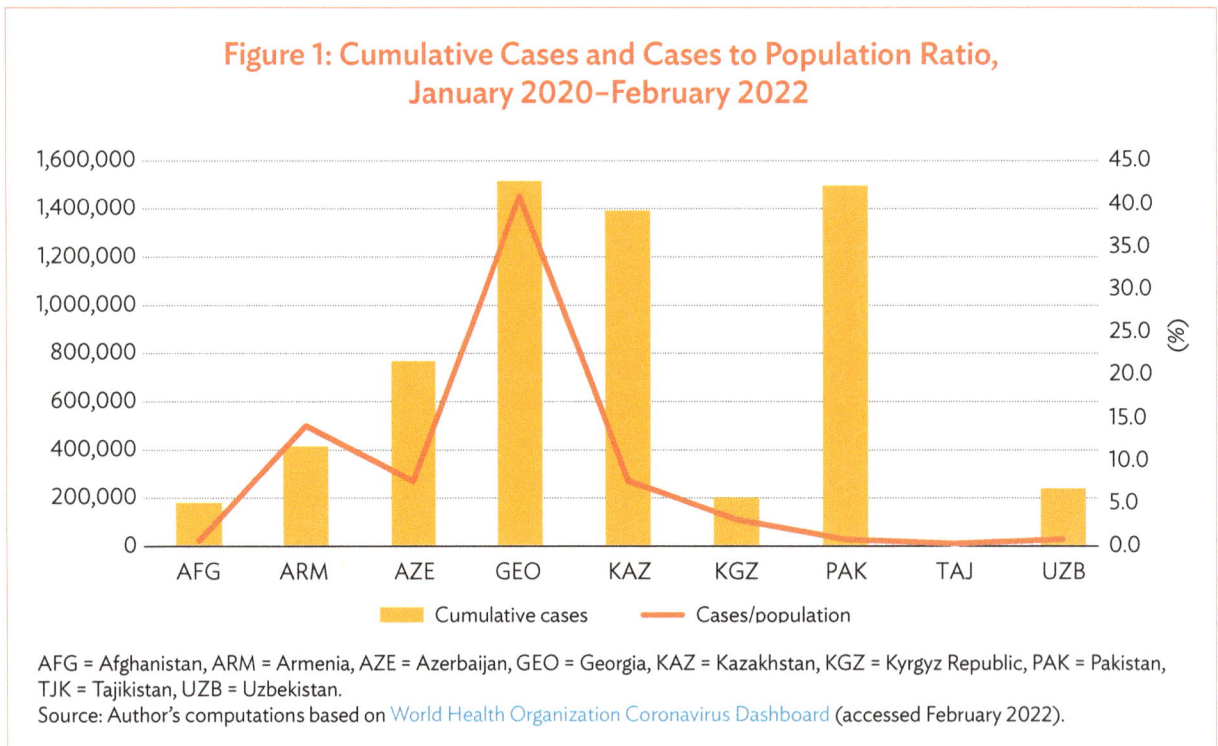

**Figure 1: Cumulative Cases and Cases to Population Ratio, January 2020–February 2022**

AFG = Afghanistan, ARM = Armenia, AZE = Azerbaijan, GEO = Georgia, KAZ = Kazakhstan, KGZ = Kyrgyz Republic, PAK = Pakistan, TJK = Tajikistan, UZB = Uzbekistan.
Source: Author's computations based on World Health Organization Coronavirus Dashboard (accessed February 2022).

In terms of deaths, Pakistan had the highest number in absolute terms (almost 30,000 as of February 2022), whereas Afghanistan had the highest rate of deaths versus cases (4.4%), followed by Armenia (2.0%) and Pakistan (2.0%) as of February 2022 (Figure 2).

**Figure 2: Cumulative Deaths and Deaths to Cases Ratio, January 2020–February 2022**

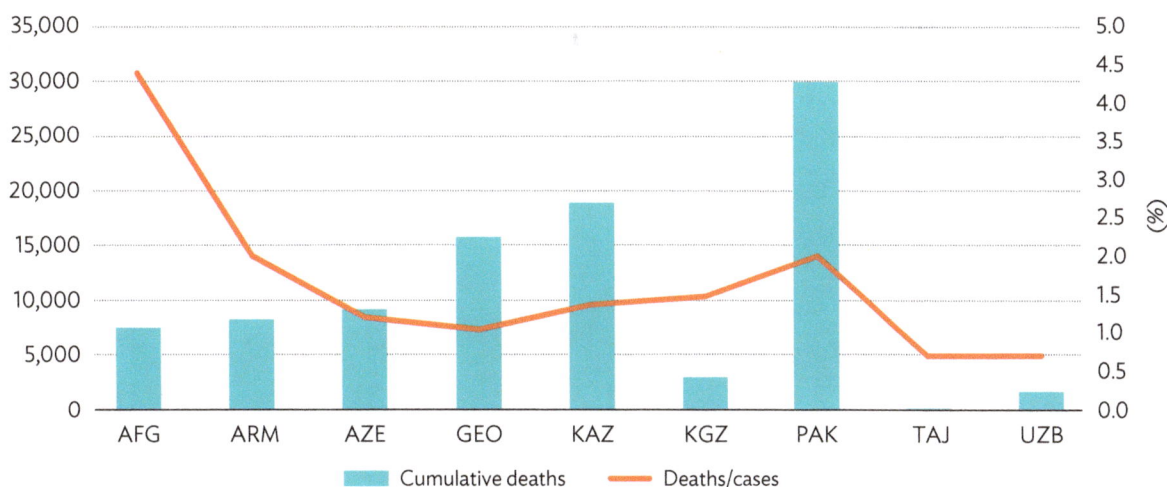

AFG = Afghanistan, ARM = Armenia, AZE = Azerbaijan, GEO = Georgia, KAZ = Kazakhstan, KGZ = Kyrgyz Republic, PAK = Pakistan, TJK = Tajikistan, UZB = Uzbekistan.
Source: Author's computations based on World Health Organization Coronavirus Dashboard (accessed February 2022).

Gendered data on COVID-19 cases and deaths is neither widely available nor kept up to date in CWA countries. Available data as of February 2022 shows that in most countries men were at a higher risk of dying if they caught COVID-19 (Figure 3).[11]

**Figure 3: Cases and Deaths by Sex/Gender**
**(%)**

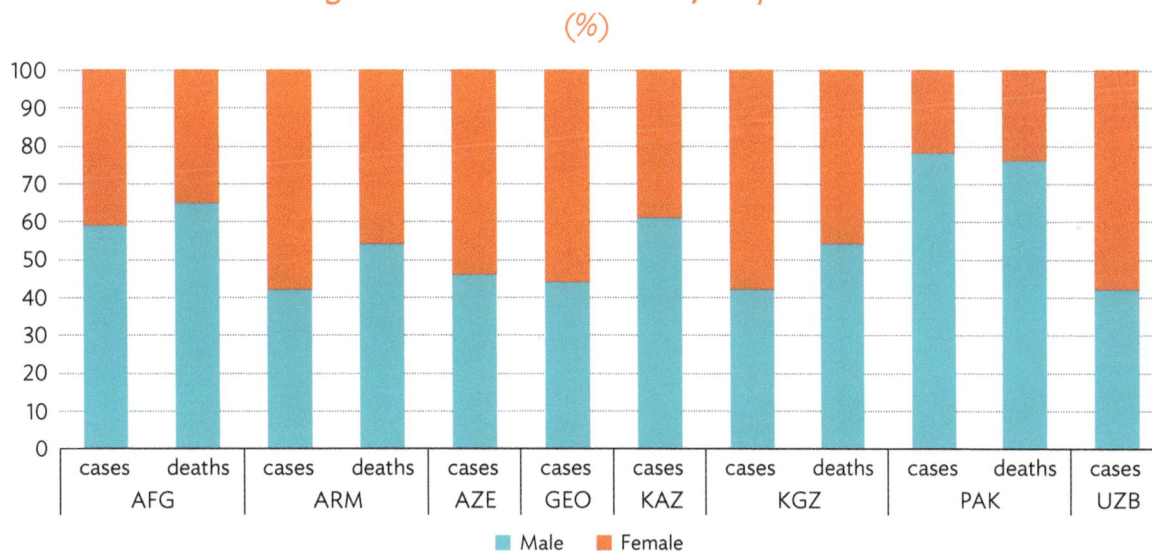

AFG = Afghanistan, ARM = Armenia, AZE = Azerbaijan, GEO = Georgia, KAZ = Kazakhstan, KGZ = Kyrgyz Republic, PAK = Pakistan, UZB = Uzbekistan.
Note: Data is relative to different time periods in each country.
Source: Author's computations, based on Global Health 50/50 (accessed February 2022).

---

[11]   Given the patchy data availability across countries and underreporting, these figures are only partially informative.

Finally, it is worth looking at the COVID-19 stringency of restrictions index.[12] The stringency index is a composite measure based on nine response indicators including school closures, workplace closures, and travel bans, scaled to a value from 0 to 100 (where 100 = strictest). If policies vary at the subnational level, the index shows the response level of the strictest subregion. Stringency of restrictions including lockdown and limitation to mobility was highest in all countries of the region in the first half of 2020, with Tajikistan showing much more limited restrictions (Figure 4). Stringency of restrictions has been in general milder throughout 2021, with significant variations among countries. In January 2022, Kazakhstan upheld the most restrictions, while Tajikistan, Afghanistan, and Pakistan in this order, had the fewest.

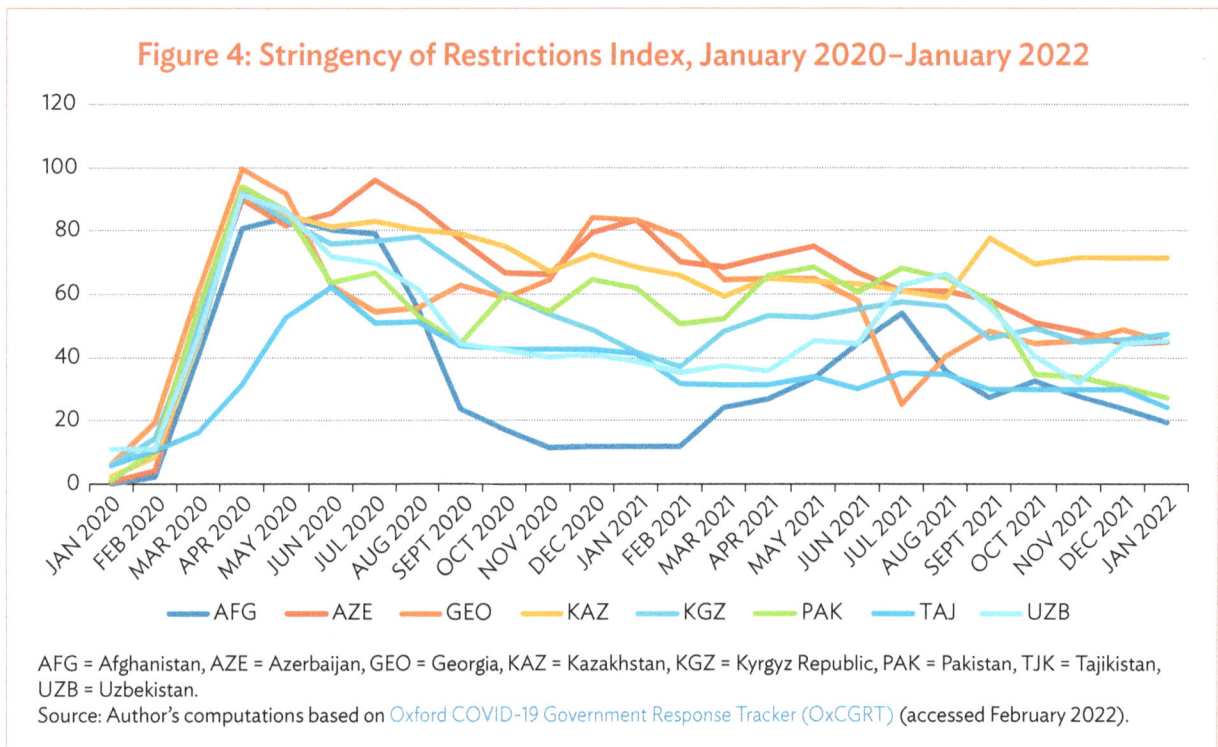

**Figure 4: Stringency of Restrictions Index, January 2020–January 2022**

AFG = Afghanistan, AZE = Azerbaijan, GEO = Georgia, KAZ = Kazakhstan, KGZ = Kyrgyz Republic, PAK = Pakistan, TJK = Tajikistan, UZB = Uzbekistan.
Source: Author's computations based on Oxford COVID-19 Government Response Tracker (OxCGRT) (accessed February 2022).

---

[12]   This index is prepared by the Blavatnik School of Government of the University of Oxford, within the framework of their Oxford COVID-19 Government Response Tracker (OxCGRT), which collects systematic information on policy measures that governments have taken to tackle COVID-19. Policy responses have been tracked since 1 January 2020 and cover more than 180 countries.

# Chapter 4

# Gender Gaps and Global Gender Indicators in Central and West Asia

Most CWA countries have passed national legislation promoting gender equality and nondiscrimination of women. However, national statistics and global gender indicators point to persistent gender-based disparities across all countries in the region.

The global indicators outlined in this section provide an overall picture of gender inequalities in CWA countries, reflecting some broad similarities but also revealing significant differences and specificities that need to be understood. Except for Afghanistan, a low-income country, all other CWA countries are classified as middle income.[13]

The **Gender Inequality Index** provides a composite score based on gender parity in education and labor markets, maternal and adolescent mortality rates, and women's parliamentary representation. The data shows that Kazakhstan (0.9) and Armenia (0.245) are the countries best placed in CWA. Kazakhstan ranks 44 and Armenia ranks 54 out of 189 countries. Afghanistan (0.66) and Pakistan (0.54) show the most marked gender inequalities in the region (Table 2).[14]

The **Gender Development Index** measures gender gaps in human development achievements based on disparities between women and men in three basic dimensions of human development—health, knowledge, and living standards—using the same component indicators as in the Human Development Index. Armenia, Georgia, and Kazakhstan rank best (Table 2) (footnote 15).

### Table 2: Gender Inequality Index and Gender Development Index, 2020

| Country | Gender Inequality Index | | Gender Development Index |
| --- | --- | --- | --- |
| | Value | Global Rank | Value |
| **Afghanistan** | 0.66 | 157 | 0.659 |
| **Armenia** | 0.25 | 54 | 0.982 |
| **Azerbaijan** | 0.32 | 73 | 0.943 |
| **Georgia** | 0.33 | 76 | 0.980 |
| **Kazakhstan** | 0.19 | 44 | 0.980 |

*continued on next page*

---

[13] Different regional groupings used internationally set Pakistan and Afghanistan in South Asia, rather than in Central Asia.
[14] UNDP. 2020. *Human Development Report 2020*. New York

Table 2 continued

| Country | Gender Inequality Index | | Gender Development Index |
| | Value | Global Rank | Value |
| --- | --- | --- | --- |
| Kyrgyz Republic | 0.37 | 82 | 0.957 |
| Pakistan | 0.54 | 135 | 0.745 |
| Tajikistan | 0.31 | 70 | 0.823 |
| Uzbekistan | 0.29 | 62 | 0.939 |

Note: The Gender Inequality Index provides a composite score based on gender parity in education and labor markets, maternal and adolescent mortality rates, and women's parliamentary representation. The Gender Development Index measures gender gaps in human development achievements based on disparities in three basic dimensions of human development—health, knowledge, and living standards—using the same component indicators as in the Human Development Index.
Source: United Nations Development Programme. 2020. *Human Development Report 2020*. New York.

Specific aspects of gender in the region can be examined by reviewing a few further basic indicators in Table 3.[15]

## Table 3: Global Gender Indicators in Central and West Asian Countries

| Country | Maternal Mortality Ratio* (Deaths per 100,000 live births) | Adolescent Birth Rate* (Births per 1,000 women ages 15–19) | Share of Seats in Parliament** (% held by women) | Population with at Least Some Secondary Education* (% ages 25 and older) | | Labor Force Participation Rate*** (% ages 15 and older) modeled International Labour Organization estimate | |
| | | | | Female | Male | Female | Male |
| | 2017 | 2015–2020 | 2022 | 2015–2019 | 2015–2019 | 2020 | 2020 |
| --- | --- | --- | --- | --- | --- | --- | --- |
| AFG | 638 | 69 | – | 13.2 | 36.9 | 16.2 | 65.6 |
| ARM | 26 | 2.5 | 35.5 | 97.3 | 97.2 | 42.0 | 62.4 |
| AZE | 26 | 55.8 | 18.3 | 93.9 | 97.5 | 59.2 | 66.6 |
| GEO | 25 | 46.4 | 19.1 | 97.2 | 98.6 | 50.7 | 69.2 |
| KAZ | 10 | 29.8 | 27.4 | 99.3 | 99.6 | 63.6 | 75.4 |
| KGZ | 60 | 32.8 | 20.5 | 99.1 | 98.3 | 41.6 | 71.0 |
| PAK | 140 | 38.8 | 20.5 | 27.6 | 45.7 | 20.6 | 77.7 |
| TAJ | 17 | 57.1 | 27.0 | 93.3 | 95.7 | 30.4 | 50.6 |
| UZB | 29 | 23.8 | 33.3 | 99.9 | 100.0 | 44.8 | 70.8 |

AFG = Afghanistan, ARM = Armenia, AZE = Azerbaijan, GEO = Georgia, KAZ = Kazakhstan, KGZ = Kyrgyz Republic, PAK = Pakistan, UZB = Uzbekistan.
Sources: *United Nations Development Programme. *Human Development Report 2020*. New York.
**Inter-Parliamentary Union Women in Parliament Ranking (as of 1 March 2022).
***World Bank. World Development Indicators (accessed February 2022).

---

[15]    The indicators in Table 3 are the same ones that are used to make up UNDP's composite Gender Inequality Index. Some of the figures presented in Table 3, specifically labor participation and political participation, are updated and more recent if compared to those used to calculate the 2020 gender inequality indexes.

The **maternal mortality ratio** in Afghanistan registered a staggering 638 maternal deaths out of 100,000 live births registered in 2017, followed by Pakistan with 140; this can be compared with Kazakhstan, where the number of deaths was 10 in the same year, and Tajikistan had 17.[16]

**Adolescent birth rates** are quite high in CWA compared to other areas in Asia, especially for Afghanistan, Azerbaijan, and Tajikistan. Rates are lowest in Armenia and Uzbekistan, which are more in line with Eastern European figures.

**Representation in parliament** varies across the region. Following 2020 elections, the composition of the Uzbek parliament changed markedly. Currently, 33.3% of seats being won by women, achieving the Beijing Platform for Action target of 30% women's representation in parliament. Likewise, elections in Armenia in 2021 resulted in 35.5% of seats going to women. The remaining countries in the CWA region fall below this target, though Kazakhstan and Tajikistan are quite close, with approximately 27% of seats held by women. Azerbaijan has the lowest proportion of parliament seats held by women at 18.3%.[17]

A systemic gender gap in **labor force participation** exists across all CWA countries, with disparities in employment rates, quality of employment, and pay scales (Table 3). Economic participation of women is relatively low compared to men's in all nine countries, with an extremely wide gap in Pakistan, where only 20.6% of employment-age women participate in the labor market compared with 77.7% of men, as well as in Afghanistan, where 16.2% of women participate in the formal labor market versus 65.6% of men. These participation rates for women are extremely low even by global comparison.[18] Azerbaijan has the smallest gender gap in labor force participation, at 59.2% of women compared to 66.6% of men.

Most CWA countries have achieved gender parity or near parity in regard to secondary education. This is partly due to the structural legacy of communism in most countries in the region. Uzbekistan has the highest figures, at 99.9% for women and 100% for men. At the other extreme are Afghanistan and Pakistan. Girls have not been allowed to attend school in Afghanistan since the Taliban takeover in 2021, while in Pakistan only 27.6% of girls attend secondary school compared with 45.7% of boys.[19]

The World Economic Forum's Global Gender Gap Index measures gender-based gaps in access to resources and opportunities relative to four categories: (i) economic participation and opportunity, (ii) educational attainment, (iii) health and survival, and (iv) political empowerment. The 2021 Gender Gap Index included data on 156 countries, including all the countries analyzed in this assessment, except for Uzbekistan (Figure 5).[20]

---

[16] At the time of writing in March 2022, the most recent comparable data on maternal mortality are relative to 2017. See United Nations Population Fund (UNFPA). 2021. *Lifetime Risk of Maternal Death in Eastern Europe and Central Asia*. Istanbul.

[17] Inter-Parliamentary Union Women in Parliament Ranking as of 1 March 2022. The indicator refers to the share of women parliamentarians in the lower or single house.

[18] Globally, the region with the lowest rate of female labor force participation is the Middle East and North Africa, excluding high income countries, at 15.4%.

[19] ADB placed its regular assistance on hold in Afghanistan effective 15 August 2021.

[20] World Economic Forum. 2021. *Global Gender Gap Report*. Geneva.

## Figure 5: Gender Gap Index, 2018–2021

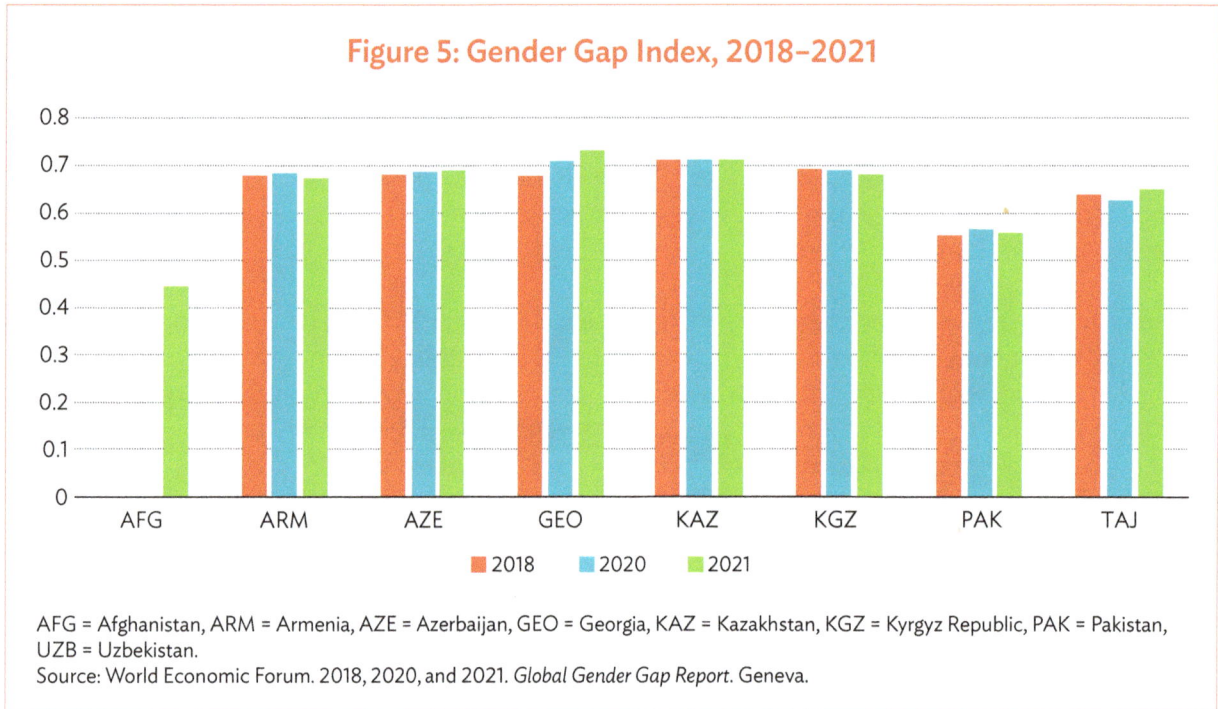

AFG = Afghanistan, ARM = Armenia, AZE = Azerbaijan, GEO = Georgia, KAZ = Kazakhstan, KGZ = Kyrgyz Republic, PAK = Pakistan, UZB = Uzbekistan.
Source: World Economic Forum. 2018, 2020, and 2021. *Global Gender Gap Report*. Geneva.

Of these countries, Georgia is ranked at 49 and Kazakhstan at 80, putting them at the lead of the CWA countries. The effects of the pandemic are still not fully visible in these figures since the 2021 index is based on 2020, as well as 2019 data. However, there is no clear upward tendency for any country, except Georgia and Tajikistan, though this is mostly due to increases in women's political representation in the parliament achieved in the 2020 elections. This may be a signal that progress toward gender equality has slowed down or even reversed.

# Chapter 5

# Gendered Impacts of COVID-19 in Central and West Asia: The Main Challenges Ahead

The gender-related observations and data collected through the stakeholder survey and desk review confirmed that CWA countries share many commonalities in terms of vulnerabilities, risks, and challenges. The three key challenges emerging as a result of the pandemic are (i) negative employment and livelihood impacts in specific sectors, with a focus on micro, small, and medium-sized enterprises (MSMEs), (ii) an overall increase in violence against women and girls (VAWG), often termed globally as the shadow pandemic; and to a lesser extent (iii) the increased burden of unpaid work on women and its connection to mental health and lower income-generating opportunities.

Other challenges that came up include the difficulties of developing an inclusive policymaking process in an emergency setting, at least in some countries, and a lack of reliable gender data required to develop gender-responsive, evidence-based policies and public investment.

Indirect health effects of the pandemic have been harder to assess given the large data gaps, globally and in CWA. There have certainly been gender-related differences in exposure, as the health workforce is mostly female in the region; access to health care, including maternal health, was also disrupted, especially at the beginning of the pandemic.

The main findings of the impact analysis follow.

## Livelihoods and Work, Including Entrepreneurship and Migration

The pandemic caused catastrophic losses in employment for women in 2020. In absolute numbers, women globally lost 54 million jobs, or 4.2% of all jobs, compared to 3% for men. Women's employment-to-population ratios declined proportionally more than men's for all country income level groups, but particularly in middle-income countries, the group to which most CWA countries belong.[21] Employment to population ratios also declined in CWA between 2019 and 2020, for both women and men (Figure 6). Existing projections show that employment for both women and men will probably recover in 2021, but at a slower speed for women, and that gender gaps will remain slightly above their 2019 levels.[22]

---

[21] Kyrgyz Republic, Pakistan, Tajikistan, and Uzbekistan are lower-middle income countries; Armenia, Azerbaijan, Georgia, and Kazakhstan are upper-middle income countries; Afghanistan is the only low-income country within CWA.

[22] International Labour Organization (ILO). 2021. *An Uneven and Gender-Unequal COVID-19 Recovery: Update on Gender and Employment Trends 2021*. Geneva.

**Figure 6: Employment to Population Ratio Female and Male, 2019 and 2020**
**(%)**

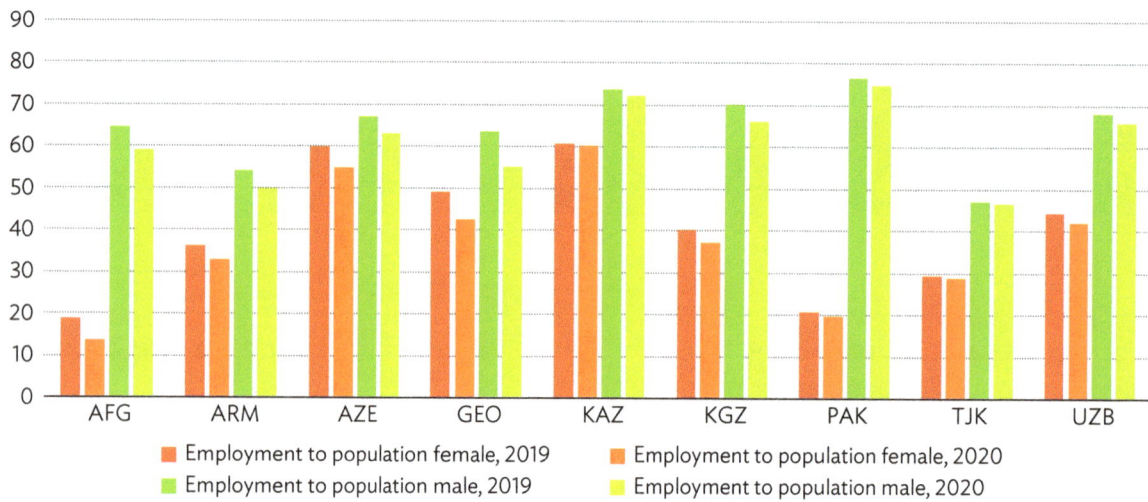

■ Employment to population female, 2019    ■ Employment to population female, 2020
■ Employment to population male, 2019    ■ Employment to population male, 2020

AFG = Afghanistan, ARM = Armenia, AZE = Azerbaijan, GEO = Georgia, KAZ = Kazakhstan, KGZ = Kyrgyz Republic, PAK = Pakistan, TJK = Tajikistan, UZB = Uzbekistan.
Source: World Bank. World Development Indicators (accessed February 2022).

Employment figures, however, do not tell the full story on gendered impacts of the pandemic because of the high share of women doing informal and unpaid work, including in the agriculture sector, and the fact that updated gender data on informal work is not widely available.

In general, women's employment in CWA is more vulnerable than men's to external shocks and crises because of the structure of labor markets and social norms restricting women's opportunities. The disproportionate impact of the pandemic on women's jobs has mainly to do with a higher vulnerability to layoffs and loss of employment, with several factors at work here.

In CWA, women are overrepresented in the services sector compared to men, and particularly in subsectors negatively affected by the pandemic; women are also overrepresented in more vulnerable types of work, like part-time, unpaid, and informal work.[23] Their chances of entering or reentering the job market may also be made harder by increased automation and digitalization of labor.

Ultimately, the vulnerability of women's work is connected to socials norms and gendered power asymmetries in CWA economies, which also show up in discriminatory practices in the workplace, including prioritizing men over women in recruitment of management positions and for career advancement or laying women off before men. Other discriminatory practices may be related to pregnancy and/or maternity, like not renewing contracts of women who are pregnant or avoiding hiring women at the height of their reproductive age, which varies somewhat culturally as well as according to social class. Discriminatory practices may also include overburdening women with certain tasks that hinge on their traditional care role, as well as disparities in salaries.

---

[23]    UN Women. 2021. *Assessing the Lights and Shadows of COVID-19: A Gender Analysis of Pandemic-Related Impacts on Women and Girls in Europe and Central Asia*. Istanbul.

This is also partly confirmed by the analysis presented in Box 2, which examines the stringency of restrictions index in conjunction with relative loss of employment for men and women separately.[24]

## Box 2: Stringency of Restrictions vs Loss of Employment

Analyzing the relation between direct and indirect effects of the pandemic is challenging due to a lack of recent and comparable quantitative gender data. However robust estimates of employment loss in all Central and West Asian countries in 2020 are available, so an analysis of its relation to the stringency of restrictions can be carried out.

As can be seen in the graphs, the value of the stringency of restrictions index in each country has been analyzed in conjunction with the relative loss of employment for men and women separately.[a] These variables are highly correlated, meaning that in countries where on average restrictions were more stringent, loss of employment was higher. Stringency of restrictions affected proportionately more women's employment than men's, confirming their higher vulnerability.[b]

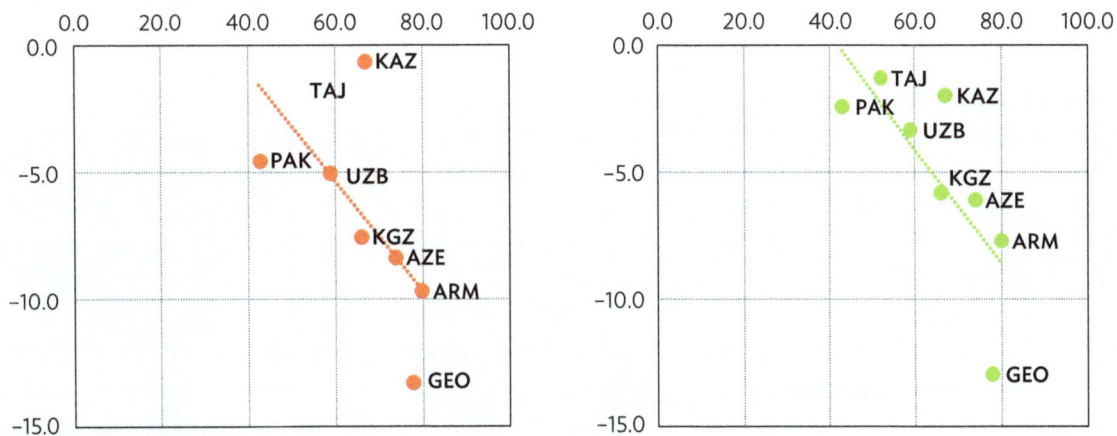

ARM = Armenia, AZE = Azerbaijan, GEO = Georgia, KAZ = Kazakhstan, KGZ = Kyrgyz Republic, PAK = Pakistan, TAJ = Tajikistan, UZB = Uzbekistan.

[a] Deriving relative employment-to-population losses for women and men requires analyzing proportional changes, going beyond percentage points differences.

[b] A multivariate linear regression could further explain the loss of employment including other variables besides stringency of restrictions.

Source: Author's computation based on World Bank Data and on Oxford COVID-19 Government Response Tracker (OxCGRT).

Women tend to work in sectors hit especially hard by COVID-19. Globally, almost 510 million or 40% of all employed women work in accommodation, food, sales, and low-wage manufacturing branches, compared with 36.6% of men (footnote 23). In most CWA countries, women also tend to work in sectors like accommodation, food service, and personal services, all hit hardest by the pandemic.[25] Agriculture also remains an important sector in many of the region's economies and contributes to a large share of female employment. In Azerbaijan, Georgia, Pakistan, and Tajikistan, agriculture accounts for more than 40% of female employment.[26]

---

[24]  Deriving relative employment-to-population losses for women and men requires analyzing proportional changes, going beyond percentage points differences. In CWA, proportional losses in employment have been greater for women in all countries except Kazakhstan.

[25]  Organisation for Economic Co-operation and Development. 2021. *Gender Gaps in Eurasia: The Daunting Effects of COVID-19*. Paris.

[26]  ILO. 2018. *Women and Men in the Informal Economy: A Statistical Picture*. Geneva.

A strikingly high number of stakeholders agreed in saying that although men were also affected by the pandemic, women were more vulnerable to its effects and have been carrying the burden of the crisis disproportionately, also despite their care role at home.

In Tajikistan many stakeholders highlighted that women's employment is particularly vulnerable compared to men's, underlining that social factors negatively affect women's mobility, education, and skills, thereby increasing their vulnerability. A survey on the impact of COVID-19 on livelihoods in Tajikistan confirmed that women's vulnerability is associated with the sectors they mostly work in and were the most affected by the pandemic. These include tourism, hotels, personal services, and catering. Data collected through this survey also shows that women are more represented among informal workers in formal sectors than men.[27]

Governmental actors in Armenia and Uzbekistan also stressed that women's employment vulnerability is because they work in hardest hit and precarious sectors including domestic work, caregiving, and agriculture work, and are often excluded from social security programs. In Uzbekistan, the importance of the "legalization" of informal workers was highlighted by governmental stakeholders, identifying this as a priority for 2022.

The vulnerability of being an informal worker in certain sectors is well-exemplified by the case of domestic workers. In Georgia, an interesting qualitative study showed that the pandemic further exacerbated the precarious nature of domestic work. Domestic workers explained that in the first phase of the pandemic, they either lost their livelihoods or had to agree to decreased compensation or less favorable job conditions. Domestic workers employed informally found it hard to receive any kind of compensation.[28]

In Azerbaijan, government stakeholders underlined that women's unemployment has risen more than men's because of the pandemic. Even though reliable data are scarce, economists estimate that informal economic activity makes up a considerable part of the country's gross domestic product (GDP) and that women's employment rate in the informal sector is much higher than men's. Some 62.0% of women in the non-agriculture sector were estimated to be in vulnerable employment in 2018, compared to 48.5.% of men.[29]

MSMEs owned by women were also particularly affected by the pandemic and associated restrictions compared to those owned by men.

In Central Asia, survey results confirmed the negative impacts of lockdown measures on services and smaller businesses. It is also clear that women-run enterprises were affected more severely, with 68% reporting suspension of activities versus 56% for businesses owned by men.[30]

In Kazakhstan, small and medium-sized enterprises (SMEs) in the services sector decreased by 6,000 units in the first 9 months of 2020, and not all SMEs started working again despite significant easing of restrictions at the end of August. The share of SMEs in Kazakhstan's 2020 GDP also

[27]   UNDP. 2020. *Impact of COVID-19 on Lives, Livelihoods and Micro, Small and Medium-Sized Enterprises (MSMEs) in Tajikistan*. New York.
[28]   UN Women. 2020. *Assessment of COVID-19's Impact on Women Employed as Domestic Workers in Georgia*. New York.
[29]   A. Valiyev. 2020. *Attaining SDG 8 in Azerbaijan: The Challenges of Economic Transformation and Job Creation*. ILO: Geneva.
[30]   UNDP. 2020. *COVID-19 and Central Asia: Socio-economic Impacts and Key Policy Considerations for Recovery*. New York.
       The report and data presented refer to 4 Central Asian economies: Kazakhstan, Kyrgyz Republic, Tajikistan, and Uzbekistan.

decreased. Meanwhile, 65.3% of female entrepreneurs stopped their businesses during lockdown, versus 53.5% of men. This relates to the sectoral structure of women's entrepreneurship, with higher shares in the wholesale and retail trade sector, which was particularly affected in the initial phase of the pandemic.

In Uzbekistan, lockdowns from March to August 2020 caused a considerable decline in the revenues of SMEs and exhausted their cash reserves. This temporarily stopped the operations of about 84,000 SMEs in the services sector, including catering, retail trade, and transport. Tourism, a critical SME job segment, was also highly affected with only 1.5 million international arrivals, a 77% reduction on 2019.[31] Women's businesses, concentrated in hardest hit sectors, were substantially affected. At the national level, 80% of individual female-owned businesses are condensed in three sectors: (i) retail trade, (ii) bakery and cooking, and (iii) sewing and tailoring. Beauty salons, clothing accessories, and Paynet copy and photo centers are also popular entrepreneurial choices for women.[32] Informants explained that one reason the three sectors are favored is that less start-up capital is needed. Moreover, there is a gender gap in terms of access to mobile devices in Uzbekistan, with men 21% more likely to have access than women; plausibly, this also contributed to the increased impact of restrictions on women's businesses.

Likewise, in Tajikistan, a UNDP survey showed that most MSMEs felt that their operations were negatively affected by the COVID-19 outbreak. Businesses in tourism and hospitality suffered losses because of border closures and travel restrictions (footnote 28). Individual entrepreneurs and enterprises in the services sector were also significantly affected, with many hairdressers or beauty salons, restaurants, and cafeterias needing to temporarily close, in a country in which female entrepreneurs are concentrated in services and catering.[33] With regard to entrepreneurship and access to credit, a civil society representative working on the ground noted that before the pandemic, women were able to use the services of banks and receive favorable loans. General restrictions, especially during the initial phase of the pandemic, limited access to resources and credit for rural women in particular.

In Western Asia, the impacts of the pandemic on women's entrepreneurship were similar.

In Armenia, an International Finance Corporation survey of women-owned enterprises showed that 80.7% of surveyed businesses experienced a reduction in revenue due to the COVID-19 outbreak. Demand for their products contracted for 62.7% of surveyed firms. At the time of the study, 69.2% of businesses still suffered from reduced income, and 52.9% still experienced lower demand for their products. Among government programs related to COVID-19 support, the eighth program businesses was a package of measures that aimed to support employees and individual entrepreneurs in the most affected areas of the private sector. Some 40.6% percent of applicants to this program agreed that it was highly beneficial for their businesses. Some 47.5% of male-owned firms had a positive assessment of the program benefits compared to 29.1% of female-owned firms, which may indicate that programs must be better tailored to the needs of female-owned MSMEs.[34]

---

[31] ADB. 2021. *Report and Recommendation of the President to the Board of Directors: Proposed Loan to the Republic of Uzbekistan for the Small and Medium-Sized Enterprises Development Program*. Manila.

[32] UNDP. 2019. *Women Entrepreneurs in Uzbekistan: Challenges and Opportunities*. New York.

[33] International Finance Corporation. 2014. In Tajikistan, Financing Boosts Women Entrepreneurs, Small Businesses.

[34] International Finance Corporation. 2021. *Women Entrepreneurship Study in Armenia*. Washington, DC.

In Azerbaijan, women entrepreneurs and owners of micro-businesses were also worse hit by the loss of cash flow and demand under lockdown. A study by UNDP noted that women led 22.5% of MSMEs, which were up to 20% more affected by COVID-19 than those led by men. Many MSMEs led by women and surveyed in the UNDP study had to close during and after the first lockdown.[35]

Belonging to a migrant female-headed household also proved to be a factor for increased economic vulnerability. Two of the world's top ten remittance recipients in terms of GDP share are in CWA, namely the Kyrgyz Republic and Tajikistan. To a lesser extent, Uzbekistan also depends on remittances, with about 2.5 million out of its approximately 35 million citizens working abroad. Labor migration from Central Asia to the Russian Federation and other countries forms the largest migration corridor in CWA and, in these three countries, most households depend on remittances. As for South Caucasus, Armenia and Georgia are among the top 10 remittance recipient economies in Asia in terms of GDP share, at over 10% each.[36]

Mobility restrictions related to the pandemic prevented seasonal agriculture workers and other migrant workers from traveling and earning incomes abroad, with a range of consequences including the contraction of remittances, affected livelihoods, aggravated household food insecurity, and hindered access to healthy diets.[37]

Data from the Kyrgyz Republic show that the initial lockdown in the Russian Federation was followed by a sharp decline in remittances received in the country, with a year-on-year fall of as much as 60% in April 2020 alone. The volume of remittances received in Uzbekistan from January to July 2020, equal to $3 billion, was 7% lower than the same period of the previous year (footnote 38).

Some 40% of international remittances are sent to rural areas, making rural households hardest hit by the decline in remittances. Many rural households are headed by women whose spouses are migrant workers, and households' livelihoods are often sustained through the (paid or unpaid) agriculture work of women and remittances of migrant spouses. Hence, as many informants noted, the real size of this impact is hard to capture as women's unpaid work is usually not registered in official surveys. A survey carried out by UNDP in Central Asia showed that income from self-employment, migrant labor, and informal jobs declined the most as a result of the COVID-19 outbreak (footnote 31).

Civil society and development partners in Tajikistan explained that many rural households were unable to obtain essential agricultural inputs and pay their taxes, so they were forced to take out additional loans because of the reduction in remittances. Support of nongovernment organizations waned because of limited contact with beneficiaries. As a consequence, the risk of girls of being undereducated and pregnant women being undernourished and unable to seek adequate health care increased.

Uzbek informants from civil society also highlighted that restrictions connected to the pandemic, like border closures, as well as decreased employment opportunities in reception countries, negatively affected households' income and entrepreneurship opportunities for women, due to the lack of capital that usually came from remittances.

---

[35]    UNDP. 2020. *Azerbaijan Socio-economic Assessment for COVID-19*. Baku.

[36]    ADB. 2020. *COVID-19 Impact on International Migration, Remittances, and Recipient Households in Developing Asia*. Manila.

[37]    Food and Agriculture Organization. 2021. *Seasonal Migration in Europe and Central Asia in the Context of the COVID-19 pandemic*. Rome.

Finally, Central Asian migrant workers in Russia risk becoming collateral victims of the ongoing Russian invasion of Ukraine. The overall level of remittances usually shrinks when Russia has an economic crisis. The International Monetary Fund resident representative to the Kyrgyz Republic said that such a decline is likely to lead to economic, fiscal, and social pressures in Central Asian countries particularly dependent on remittances.[38]

# Violence Against Women and Girls and Indirect Health Impacts

An increasingly diverse set of studies has linked the COVID-19 pandemic with increases in VAWG.[39] As a development partner underlined, pandemic response measures, which included isolation, social distancing, and restrictions on movement, created the very conditions under which perpetrators are freer to use violence.

Stakeholders in CWA countries and across all sectors identified increases in VAWG as a main pandemic impact in their context. Studies that explored dynamics around violence against women and children in the COVID-19 context highlighted economic stressors, low social support, lack of employment, substance use, poor mental health, and younger age as salient risk factors associated with intimate partner violence; parenting stress, job loss, and lack of support and perceived control were identified as salient risk factors associated with violence against children, in different settings.[40]

In CWA countries, VAWG is not clearly condemned due to prevalent social and cultural norms. For instance, more than 60% of women in Tajikistan and about 80% of women in Afghanistan believe that husbands are justified in beating their wife for some specific reasons (Figure 7).

A rapid gender assessment carried out in the Kyrgyz Republic at the onset of the pandemic showed that by May 2020 violence levels had increased by 65% compared to the same period in 2019. While 41% of women said that they knew where to seek help for instances of domestic violence, only 33% said that they would actually seek help.[41] According to another survey carried out in 2021, which specifically analyzed the impact of COVID-19 on the well-being and safety of women in the Kyrgyz Republic, 47% of the surveyed women said they knew a woman who had experienced a form of violence against women in their lifetime or had themselves experienced violence (including physical violence, denial of basic needs, sexual harassment, restrictions, or verbal abuse).[42]

---

[38] C.S. Kasturi. 2022. The Russia–Ukraine Crisis is Squeezing Central Asian Economies. *Al Jazeera*. 16 February.

[39] S. Bourgault et al. 2021. Violence Against Women and Children During COVID-19—One Year On and 100 Papers In. *Centre for Global Development Note*. April.

[40] A. Peterman and M. O'Donnell. 2020. COVID-19 and Violence against Women and Children: A Third Research Round Up for the 16 Days of Activism. Centre for Global Development Note. December.

[41] Social Technologies Agency and Siar Research and Consulting. 2020. *COVID-19 Impacts on Livelihoods of Women and Men in the Kyrgyz Republic*. UN Women: Bishkek.

[42] UN Women. 2022. *Measuring the Shadow Pandemic: Violence Against Women During COVID-19. Country Report: Kyrgyzstan*. New York. Due to the remote nature of this survey, indirect questions were asked as proxy indicators of violence against women, meaning it was not possible to distinguish respondent experiences from those of other women in their community or whether this experience occurred within or outside of the household. Therefore, while data from this study should not be interpreted as prevalence data, it nevertheless provides critical information on the impact of COVID-19 on women's perception of well-being and safety.

**Figure 7: Women Who Believe a Husband is Justified in Beating His Wife
(Any of Five Reasons)
(%)**

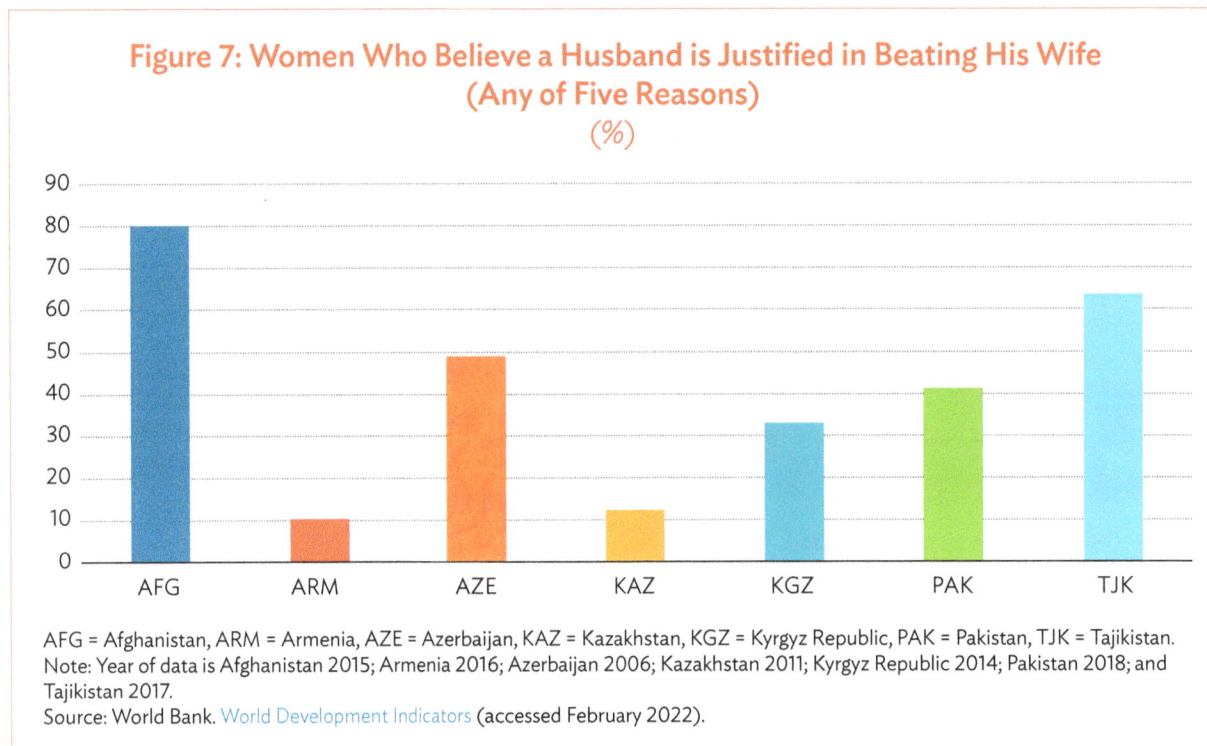

AFG = Afghanistan, ARM = Armenia, AZE = Azerbaijan, KAZ = Kazakhstan, KGZ = Kyrgyz Republic, PAK = Pakistan, TJK = Tajikistan.
Note: Year of data is Afghanistan 2015; Armenia 2016; Azerbaijan 2006; Kazakhstan 2011; Kyrgyz Republic 2014; Pakistan 2018; and Tajikistan 2017.
Source: World Bank. World Development Indicators (accessed February 2022).

Similar assessments carried out in Azerbaijan also showed that men and women experienced an increase in domestic violence from the beginning of the pandemic. The reduction in household incomes and the negative impact on psychological health and well-being caused by restrictive measures are likely to have triggered an escalation of intra-family tensions and violence.[43] It is worth noting that before the pandemic, approximately one in three women (32.1%) reported experiencing physical violence in their lifetime in Azerbaijan.[44]

In Pakistan, respondents to a survey carried out in Punjab and Sindh in July and August 2020 reported an increase in incidences of threats of physical violence (40%) and of physical assault from spouses (46%).[45] Moreover, 14% of surveyed women knew someone in their community who was threatened with physical harm by their husband, 19% knew someone who was physically assaulted by her husband, and 27% knew of cases where children were beaten by their parents (footnote 7).

Development partners in Pakistan also stressed that the rate of VAWG increased significantly due to loss of livelihoods and restrictions, highlighting the importance of a change of the narrative in the country. An article analyzing the representation of domestic violence in the media during the pandemic also shed light on the need to change biased discourses on violence that take a masculine, hegemonic perspective, conveying the meaning that women are voiceless and lack agency. However, from another point of view, the review of these articles also confirmed that domestic violence is emerging as a silent pandemic in Pakistan, posing a serious challenge to society and the state.[46]

[43]   UNFPA and UN Women. 2020. *Rapid Gender Assessment of the Impact of COVID-19 on the Lives of Women and Men in Azerbaijan.* Baku.
[44]   UNFPA et al. 2018. *Gender Equality and Gender Relations in Azerbaijan: Current Trends and Opportunities. Findings from the Men and Gender Equality Survey.* Baku.
[45]   F. Bari et al. 2020. *COVID-19 and the New Normal for Women in the Economy: Case for Pakistan.* Islamabad: The Asia Foundation.
[46]   R. Ali and A. Khalid. 2021. COVID-19 and Domestic Violence in Pakistan: An Analysis of the Media Perspective. *Journal of International Women's Studies.* 22 (12). 98–114.

According to data from the Ministry of Internal Affairs in Georgia, the number of restraining orders issued in 2019 was 10,266.[47] In 2020 it was 10,321 and in 2021 9,376. Violence therefore did not increase in Georgia during the pandemic. However, further studies showed that this is probably due to underreporting, as women feared that even if they appealed to help services or called the police, their problems would not be prioritized due to the burden of pandemic-related work. Some 56% of victims declared that they did not call 112 (the dedicated help telephone line) to report a violent incident, citing lack of trust, lack of awareness, and long waiting times.[48]

In regard to other aspects of women's health and well-being, publicly available gender-disaggregated data are still incomplete. Some of the largest data gaps are in sexual and reproductive health care and they are particularly marked in Asian countries.[49]

While assessing the pandemic's impact on women's health faces significant limitations, particularly in CWA, some interesting conclusions can still be deduced. In terms of maternal health, globally, around 200 million women are pregnant each year and nearly half (90 million) give birth in facilities. Routine health care services were interrupted due to the pandemic, especially in countries with weaker health systems, threatening global progress toward reducing maternal and child morbidity and mortality. Emerging evidence indicates that many countries continue to record substantial reduction in health care use by pregnant women while evidence on birth outcomes has been mixed.[50]

In regard to sexual and reproductive health, since the beginning of the pandemic, there have been significant concerns about how COVID-19 would impact progress in the family planning space. Evidence currently available shows that sexual and reproductive health care delivery was disrupted by COVID-19.[51] Effects are however highly variable across national and subnational settings, with assessments relying on a variety of data sources and methods. In Pakistan, as one CSO underlined, women were reluctant to visit hospitals for ante- and post-natal check-ups and deliveries, especially in the initial phases of the pandemic. According to some informants, delivery cases in some hospitals were not accepted or admitted due to fear by service providers of contracting the virus.[52] Moreover, outpatient departments in most hospitals were closed and resources were diverted to treat COVID-19 patients and contain the spread.

Existing evidence also points to a stronger impact of the pandemic on women's mental health compared to men. A survey conducted in Georgia showed that gender and the presence of persons with disabilities in households were predictors of whether a respondent would report deteriorated mental health.[53] In the Kyrgyz Republic, according to a survey carried out after the first wave of

[47]  Government of Georgia. Ministry of Internal Affairs. Public Information. Statistics on Violence Against Women and Domestic Violence.

[48]  UNDP. 2021. The Challenges in the Provision of Services to Female Victims of Domestic Violence by the Ministry of Internal Affairs during the COVID-19 Pandemic. Tbilisi.

[49]  L. S. Flor, et al. 2022. Quantifying the Effects of the COVID-19 Pandemic on Gender Equality on Health, Social, and Economic Indicators: A Comprehensive Review of Data from March, 2020, to September, 2021. The Lancet. 399. 2381–97.

[50]  C. Krubiner et al. 2021. Addressing the COVID-19 Crisis's Indirect Health Impacts for Women and Girls. Centre for Global Development Working Paper. No. 577. Washington DC: Center for Global Development.

[51]  A. Awofeso et al. 2021. COVID-19 and Women and Girls' Health in Low and Middle-Income Countries: An Updated Review of the Evidence. Centre for Global Development Policy Paper. No. 234. Washington DC: Center for Global Development.

[52]  I. Kamram et al. 2020. Reproductive Health Care in the Time of COVID-19: Perspectives of Poor Women and Service Providers from Rahim Yar Khan, Punjab. Islamabad: Population Council.

[53]  UN Women, UNDP, and UNFPA. 2021. Second Wave of Covid-19. The Rapid Gender Assessment of the COVID-19 Situation in Georgia. New York.

COVID-19, the proportion of people who said their emotional and mental health had worsened during the pandemic was 21.6%. For some vulnerable groups, like women survivors of violence and women living with HIV, this figure was at least four times as high (footnote 42).

COVID-19 impacts contributing to gendered indirect health effects were identified through a global review of evidence (footnote 8). Some were discussed by key CWA stakeholders in interviews.

First, gender-related differences in exposure were underlined. In CWA, as in most other regions, the health workforce tends to be mostly female. More female health workers were therefore exposed to psychological and physical distress. Additionally, women were also more exposed to food insecurity and undernutrition, which tends to happen in most crisis or disaster settings.

Second, the pandemic affected women's health behavior in terms of increased avoidance of health facilities due to fears of the virus, as well as in terms of changes in pregnancy intention and sex behaviour. Access to health services was also impacted by limited transportation during lockdowns, human resources being diverting to COVID-19, and closure or reduction of hours of some facilities. This seemed to be more the case at the beginning of the pandemic. Surveys carried out in Georgia showed that the proportion of those who found it difficult to obtain medical help declined by 10% with the second wave of COVID-19 in October 2020 compared to May 2020, when 30% of surveyed people said that they experienced difficulties (footnote 54).

Finally, women's health was disproportionately affected by COVID-19 due to gender-biased health systems that de-prioritize certain sexual and reproductive health services seen as "non-essential" services or depart from respectful maternal care through restrictive policies. In Azerbaijan for example, special internal protocols were quickly developed for managing births, although these protocols had to be reviewed as they interrupted early initiation of breastfeeding (footnote 36). Relying on telehealth and e-health adaptations may also affect women as gender gaps in mobile and internet use may be overlooked.

## Unpaid Care and Domestic Work

One of the main effects of the COVID-19 pandemic has been to deepen but also reveal existing gender inequalities. This is especially the case for disparities that have to do with the distribution of unpaid care and domestic work. Lockdowns and restrictions on mobility at the beginning of the pandemic as well as school closures that continued at later stages revealed that in most households, women are still disproportionately in charge of care and domestic work.

In most CWA countries, on average schools were only fully open for half of the school year or less between February 2020 and December 2021, though this varied somewhat in the region, as in Azerbaijan and Pakistan schools were only fully open for about 20% of the school year, whereas in Tajikistan, schools never closed (Figure 8).

Evidence available to date has not shown differential impacts of school closures on boys and girls in terms of learning loss and dropping out. However, a global review of over 40 studies that document learning loss, dropout, or both, found largely consistent evidence of average learning loss across countries, with poorer students performing worse. Dropout rates vary dramatically across settings but are highest

## Figure 8: School Closures in Central and West Asian Countries, February 2020–December 2021
### (%)

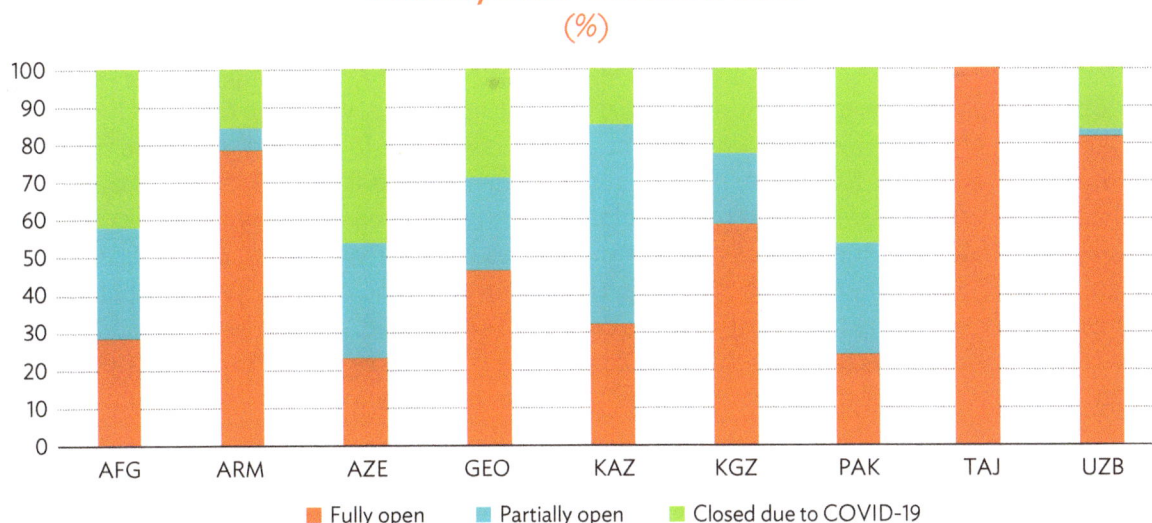

■ Fully open    ■ Partially open    ■ Closed due to COVID-19

AFG = Afghanistan, ARM = Armenia, AZE = Azerbaijan, GEO = Georgia, KAZ = Kazakhstan, KGZ = Kyrgyz Republic, PAK = Pakistan, TAJ = Tajikistan, UZB = Uzbekistan.

Note: The category partially open means that schools were: (a) open/closed in certain regions only; and/or (b) open/closed for some grade levels/age groups only; and/or (c) open but with reduced in-person class time, combined with distance learning (hybrid approach). For Afghanistan this category includes schools where girls are not allowed to attend.

Source: Author's computation based on United Nations Educational, Scientific and Cultural Organization COVID 19 Education Response Dashboard.

among older children.[54] The situation is therefore worrisome and even though there is currently not enough evidence of significantly different gendered impacts, policymakers and practitioners should look at lessons from past crises and epidemics to address the specific challenges faced by girls.[55] School closures have contributed to an increase in unpaid care work (UCW), particularly for women and girls.

Since time-use surveys in CWA countries are not carried out routinely, updated data on time use that would make it possible to assess changes in unpaid work is not readily available.[56] However, existing data, including from rapid gender assessments carried out by UN Women in various CWA countries, confirmed that the closure of schools and childcare facilities placed additional burdens on women, whose responsibilities caring for family members, both well and sick, increased (footnote 24). As a result, women had less time to engage in economic activities and leisure activities.[57] This increase has been identified as an important gendered impact of the pandemic by several sources, including by most stakeholders in CWA, especially for women in urban areas and women who worked remotely.

---

[54]   A recent review [L. Flor et al. 2022. Quantifying the Effects of the COVID-19 Pandemic on Gender Equality on Health, Social, and Economic Indicators: A Comprehensive Review of Data from March, 2020, to September, 2021. *The Lancet*. 399. 2381–97] aimed at quantifying the effects of the COVID-19 pandemic on gender equality globally only mentioned one multinational source of data for the impacts on schooling. This source was based on a survey of a relatively small and non-representative sample.

[55]   Plan International. COVID-19 School Closures Around the World Will Hit Girls Hardest. 31 March 2020.

[56]   According to the UN Statistics Division, the last time-use survey in Armenia was carried out in 2008; Azerbaijan in 2008; Kazakhstan in 2012; Kyrgyz Republic in 2015; Pakistan in 2007. In remaining CWA countries, national level time-use surveys have not been carried out yet.

[57]   UN Regional Coordination Mechanism. 2020. *COVID-19 and Social Protection in Europe and Central Asia*. Venice.

While the mental health impacts of increased care burdens are yet to be assessed, though many informants have highlighted them, the linkage with decreased income-generating opportunities and labor participation is already evident. The specificities of impacts of the pandemic on women's UCW in rural areas have not been sufficiently analyzed yet.

The double or triple burden of UCW during the pandemic applies to women in different income and social groups, including professional women and gender advocates. In line with evidence from other global regions, an Armenian researcher pointed out that increased loads of UCW affected the capacity of women in universities and research organizations of doing research and publishing. Her first-hand testimony highlighted that the work of male colleagues was not nearly as affected. Likewise, a gender advocate from Georgia underlined that when activists moved to the online space, they had to face new challenges linked to digital security and so-called "Zoom fatigue," as well as stress and burnout. She said, "During the pandemic, women activists had more stress, more tension, more responsibilities, and they also had to serve their cause digitally."[58]

In the Kyrgyz Republic, pre-pandemic time-use surveys by the National Statistical Committee show that women spend slightly less time on paid work than men, but they spend 3.6 times more time on unpaid domestic work than men and 2.0 times more on childcare. The closure of schools and other educational institutions for quarantine became an additional burden, particularly for teachers. They were forced to quickly switch to online teaching without any training. Psychological stress, the need to provide for their families, and increased domestic workloads were worsened by the demands posed by their job, for which they had no skills or even basic technical equipment (footnote 42).

Pre-pandemic studies showed that in Georgia, employed women spend 42 hours weekly on care work while unemployed women spend 45 hours. Women spend about three times more time on UCW than men, who only spend approximately 15 hours on it per week (footnote 59). An assessment of the second wave of the pandemic conducted in Georgia showed that, unlike in the previous wave, the burden of unpaid domestic and care work increased similarly for women and men. Childcare however remains largely a task for which women are primarily responsible and women are more involved than men in almost every domestic chore: 47% of men are never involved in cleaning, 43% said they never cook, and 33% are never involved in childcare. On the contrary, only a few women report not doing domestic chores (footnote 54).

This anecdotal evidence highlights that the increase of UCW was particularly felt by categories of women who are already in the care sector in its broader definition, i.e., teachers, activists, and gender advocates.

Finally, as a development partner in Pakistan said, the pandemic has highlighted that the interventions of development organizations have not really penetrated the domestic space and the unequal division of labor among genders.

---

[58]    Key informant interview.

# Decision-Making and Public Finance Management

The gendered impacts of the pandemic on decision-making and public finance management are still to be fully understood, given the specific and varying timelines of political and electoral processes in the region. Moreover, many other issues are currently affecting decision-making mechanisms, including tensions in different areas of CWA and the Russian invasion of Ukraine.

Parliamentarian elections held in some CWA countries (Georgia, Tajikistan, and Uzbekistan) in 2020 and 2021 resulted in an improvement in terms of women's representation. However, the crisis management structures set up to fight the pandemic, the so-called COVID-19 task forces, were mostly led by and made up of men. The composition of these commissions, created especially but not exclusively at the start of the pandemic, paints quite an unequal picture. Available data shows that 13 out of 15 task forces established in CWA countries were led by men; an Interagency Commission in Georgia and one other task force in Tajikistan were led by women.[59] Most of these task forces also mainly comprised men, with women's representation well below 30% in most cases. Two task forces, the State Commission in Tajikistan and the IT Working Group in Armenia, were led by and comprised exclusively men (Table 4). A distinct gender imbalance was also present in many European COVID-19 task forces, hence it seems that appropriate representation or diversity in crisis management has yet to be achieved in many global regions.[60]

## Table 4: COVID-19 Task Forces

| Country | Task Force Name | Sector | No. of Men | No. of Women | Gender of Leader |
|---------|----------------|--------|------------|--------------|------------------|
| AFG | Emergency Preparedness Response (EPR) - COVID-19 Sub Committee | Public health | ... | ... | Male |
| AFG | High Committee for Emergency Management | Multisector | ... | ... | Male |
| ARM | IT Working Group for Modelling Spread of Coronavirus (unofficial name) | Public health | 12 | 0 | ... |
| ARM | Interdepartmental Commission for Coordinating the Prevention of the Spread of the New Coronavirus | Public health | 10 | 4 | Male |
| AZE | Task Force under the Cabinet of Ministers | Multisector | 33 | 1 | Male |
| GEO | Interagency Coordination Council | Multisector | 10 | 4 | Male |
| GEO | Interagency Coordination Commission on the Introduction of the COVID-19 Vaccination in Georgia | Multisector | 7 | 4 | Female |
| KAZ | State Commission for Ensuring the State of Emergency | Enforcement | 22 | 0 | Male |
| KAZ | Interdepartmental Commission on Prevention of the Emergence and Spread of Coronavirus Infection | Multisector | ... | ... | Male |

*continued on next page*

---

59 UNDP. COVID-19 Global Gender Response Tracker Database (accessed 28 February 2022).
60 Italy for example initially had a task force made up of 20 men; Hungary had only one woman out of 16 members; France's task force had 3 women in a 13-person committee. See: European Institute for Gender Equality. 2021. *Gender Equality and the Socio-Economic Impact of the COVID-19 Pandemic*. Vilnius.

Table 4 *continued*

| Country | Task Force Name | Sector | No. of Men | No. of Women | Gender of Leader |
|---------|-----------------|--------|-----------|-------------|------------------|
| KGZ | Operational headquarters for combating the spread of coronavirus infection and the spread of tis consequences | Multisector | ... | ... | Female |
| PAK | Emergency Core Committee for COVID-19 | Public health | 11 | 1 | Male |
| TJK | Inter-Agency Standing Committee (IASC) to prevent and response to COVID-19 | Multisector | 29 | 3 | Male and female (cochairs) |
| TJK | Inter-Agency Task Force on Public Engagement and Raising Awareness among the Population | Multisector | ... | ... | Female |
| TJK | Republican Headquarters for Combating COVID-19 | Multisector | ... | ... | Male |
| UZB | Special Republican Commission for Combating the Coronavirus | Public health | ... | ... | Male |
| UZB | Republican Anti-Crisis Commission | Economic | ... | ... | Male |

AFG = Afghanistan, ARM = Armenia, AZE = Azerbaijan, GEO = Georgia, KAZ = Kazakhstan, KGZ = Kyrgyz Republic, PAK = Pakistan, TJK = Tajikistan, UZB = Uzbekistan.
Sources: United Nations Development Programme. COVID-19 Global Gender Response Tracker Database; and for Kyrgyz Republic, ADB staff in-country.

The pandemic also shed light on existing imbalances in regard to gender responsive policymaking, especially in South Caucasus countries, where civil society and to a lesser extent development partners stressed that the policymaking process should be more inclusive and consultative, to promote gender equality.

CSOs in Georgia mentioned that women from civil society do not have enough opportunities to be engaged in the decision-making process, citing their experience in the environmental protection policy area among others, while high level development partners explained that social assistance emergency measures developed by the government could have benefited from their gender expertise if consulted. In Pakistan, civil society representatives expressed concerns along similar lines, highlighting that closures and other restrictions associated with the pandemic prevented meaningful coordination between CSOs and the government, exacerbating some challenges that vulnerable groups face, including for survivors of violence against women. An Armenian civil society representative added that in a recent meeting with a governmental entity, they found it hard to reach a shared understanding of how digitalization reforms are connected to gender issues.

Detailed data on gender responsiveness of public budgets that were committed after the outbreak of the pandemic would serve as an excellent indication of the priority given to gender issues in different countries; however these data do not yet exist, mostly due to the general lack of reliable gender data already noted. Limited data availability and comparability, as well as gaps in data granularity (disaggregation by sex, ethnicity etc.) are well-documented problems, both in the region and globally.[61] Limited gender data was identified as a priority problem by many key stakeholders across CWA and, even though it is a crosscutting issue, it particularly affects decision-making, as it limits the possibility

---

[61]    ADB. 2021. *Key Indicators for Asia and the Pacific 2021*. Manila; and ILO, UN Women, and World Bank. 2021. *Strengthening Gender Measures and Data in the COVID-19 Era: An Urgent Need for Change*. Geneva.

of developing evidence-based effective policy. In addition, it should be noted that the wealth of data collection initiatives and rapid assessments carried out during the first wave of COVID-19 in 2020 was not matched by similar efforts in 2021, which speaks to the lack of continuity in the production of gender data. Finally, a high-level development partner noted that inter-institutional coordination on different types of gender data production initiatives needs to improve.

# Intersecting Vulnerabilities

Intersecting vulnerabilities came up in all priority areas. The extent of these different vulnerabilities varies widely across CWA and within countries themselves. For many types of vulnerabilities, the problem with data granularity means that painting a clear picture of the disadvantages of different social groups is not always easy. However, existing data, including case studies and key stakeholder interviews carried out for this assessment, highlight how some specific vulnerable groups across the region were affected.

In regard to women's economic security, women who are informal/unpaid workers or head migrant households are particularly vulnerable to economic shocks. In some Central Asian countries (Kyrgyz Republic, Tajikistan, and Uzbekistan), where up to one in three households has a migrant member, female-headed migrant households have been especially affected by the pandemic.

Likewise, women from ethnic minorities and displaced communities face increased risks in crisis situations across the region: in South Caucasus this includes persons who were displaced by external conflicts as well as the internal civil wars of the last decades.[62] In Georgia, one survey carried out during the COVID-19 pandemic showed that ethnic minorities and rural women had higher chances of being economically inactive (footnote 54).

Vulnerability of rural women, ethnic minorities, displaced people, and persons with disabilities, was also evident in terms of the impact of the pandemic on their access to health care and exposure to VAWG. Women with disabilities specifically faced even greater inequalities in accessing health care during the pandemic due to inaccessible health information and environments, as well as selective medical guidelines and protocols that may have magnified the discrimination they face in health care provision.[63] For girls and boys with disabilities, access to education was particularly challenging. Likewise, stakeholders in Georgia and Tajikistan stressed that rural women have faced increased challenges to access health centers due to the (temporary) decline of the offer of health services during the pandemic, as well as the reduction in already scarce transport options.

In regard to VAWG, it is also important to underline that age is an important vulnerability factor, and studies show that with COVID-19, adolescents and children have become even more exposed to traditional harmful practices like child marriage. This issue was raised in interviews by stakeholders from Azerbaijan and Georgia, but available data shows it is a persistent practice in Afghanistan, the Kyrgyz Republic, Pakistan, and other Central Asian countries.[64] According to the United Nations

---

[62]  ADB. 2018. *Georgia: Country Gender Assessment*. Manila; ADB. 2019. *Armenia: Country Gender Assessment*. Manila; and ADB. 2019. *Azerbaijan: Country Gender Assessment*. Manila.

[63]  United Nations Educational, Scientific and Cultural Organization. 2021. *Disability Inclusive COVID-19 Response: Best Practices*. Paris.

[64]  UNFPA. *Child Marriage in Eastern Europe and Central Asia: Regional Overview*. Istanbul; and *Girls Not Brides*. Kyrgyz Republic.

Children's Fund (UNICEF), child marriages are surging in Asia and other developing countries, raising concerns that the international community may miss its goal of ending the practice by 2030 as pandemic-related causalities surge.[65]

Finally, lesbian, gay, bisexual, transgender, queer or questioning, and intersex (LGBTQI) communities have also proven to be especially vulnerable to crisis, in regard to access to economic opportunities and adequate health care, as well as in terms of the risk of being victims of violence. A study from Georgia showed that the COVID-19 pandemic had serious negative effects on LGBTQI people involved in informal labor, especially transgender sex workers, but their specific needs were not addressed.[66]

[65]   UNICEF. 2021. 10 Million Additional Girls at Risk of Child Marriage Due to COVID-19 – UNICEF. News release. 8 March.

[66]   N. M. Tabidze and L. Gvishiani. 2021. *Employment and Labour Rights of LGBTQI Community in the Context of COVID-19 Pandemic*. Tbilisi: Equality Movement.

# Chapter 6

# COVID-19 Response in Central and West Asia: A Gender Perspective

## Policy Response to COVID-19 in Central and West Asia

Responses taken by governments worldwide to tackle the COVID-19 pandemic can and should be analyzed with a gender perspective. The COVID-19 Global Gender Response Tracker was developed by UNDP and other international partners to monitor and highlight those that have integrated a gender lens. It analyzes policy measures that address women's economic and social security, including UCW, the labor market, and violence against women.[67] The tracker provides guidance for policymakers and evidence for advocates to better integrate gender in COVID-19 policy response.

This global policy tracker uses specific operational definitions of gender sensitivity for the policies it analyzes. Social protection and labor market measures are defined as gender-sensitive if they target women's economic security or address unpaid care, or if they target specific occupations where women are overrepresented (e.g., garment industry workers in some countries, domestic workers, school teachers, health and long-term care workers). Fiscal and economic measures are considered gender sensitive if they provide support to female-dominated sectors of the economy, on the assumption that this is likely to protect women's employment and thereby their economic security. VAWG measures on the other hand are gender sensitive by definition, as they promote women's rights to live a life free from violence.[68]

The analysis of initiatives carried out by governments in CWA in response to COVID-19 and tracked by this global database up to November 2021 shows that only about a third of the 232 policy measures implemented were gender sensitive (Figure 9). These comprise 51 VAWG measures that were taken in the region to strengthen services, raise awareness, or integrate VAWG in COVID-response plans, among other types of measures. It is interesting to note that most VAWG measures in the region (30 out of 51) were aimed at strengthening services, especially through the expansion and opening of shelters—e.g., in Kazakhstan, local government and community offices provided shelters to support the survivors of violence during the quarantine period in all regions—and the creation or expansion of

---

[67]  UNDP and UN Women. *COVID-19 Global Gender Response Tracker. Methodological Note*.

[68]  The operational definitions of gender sensitivity of measures used by this tracker are broader than other definitions found in the literature (see Box 1). VAWG measures, or other initiatives and/or policies that target specifically women or certain groups of women to revert structural gender inequalities, can be considered gender responsive and/or transformative as they address the root causes of gender equality, hence they are also gender sensitive. For measures that have other goals and take place in different development sectors and integrate a gender perspective, the line between what is considered gender sensitive in operational definitions of this tracker and what it considered gender responsive or gender transformative based on definitions given in Box 1 is less clear-cut.

**Figure 9: Gender Sensitivity of Policy Response to COVID-19 in Central and West Asia (%)**

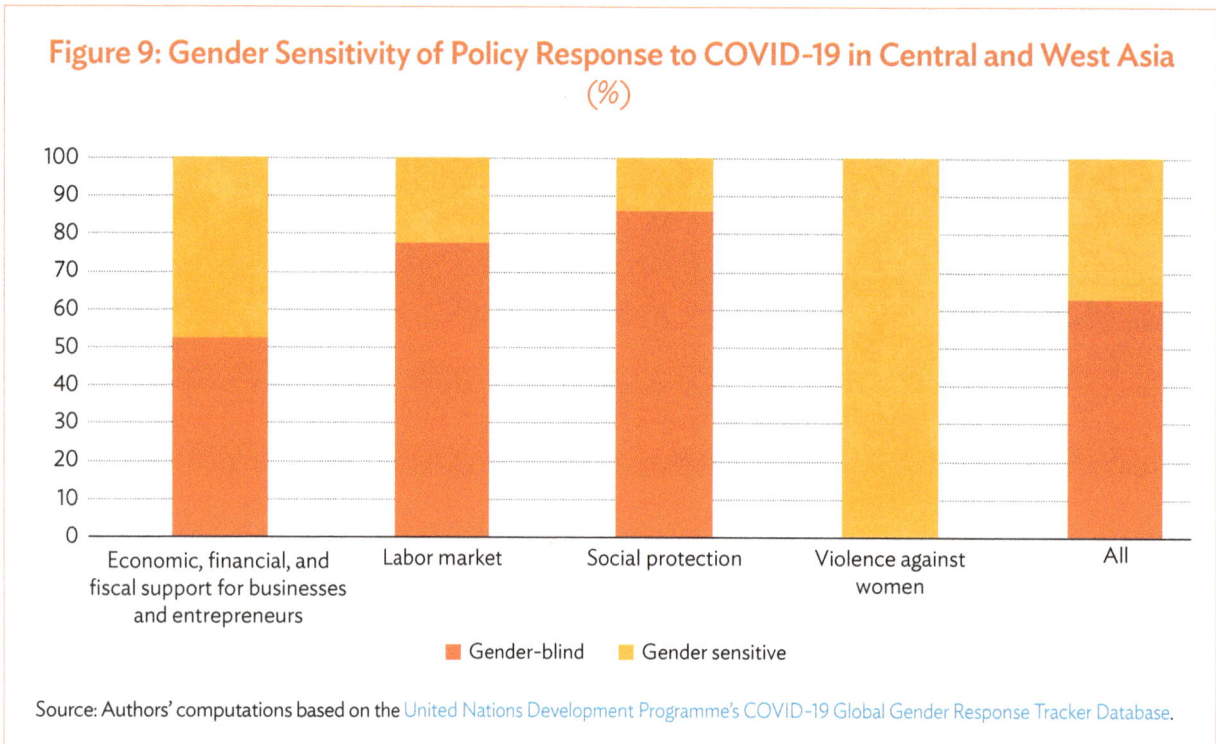

Source: Authors' computations based on the United Nations Development Programme's COVID-19 Global Gender Response Tracker Database.

hotlines and reporting mechanisms. Among these, in the Kyrgyz Republic the dedicated 117 helpline for gender-based violence survivors was set up to provide survivors with critical psychological first aid, psychosocial support, case management, and access to safety, medical care, and justice. In Armenia, the existing 114 helpline, operated by the Ministry of Labour and Social Affairs and providing, among other services, assistance to domestic violence survivors, was made to operate daily around the clock. In Kazakhstan, women could use a code phrase in grocery stores, shops, and pharmacies (including by phone) to signal the incidence of domestic violence and the need to inform the police immediately. Finally, in Pakistan at the end of 2020, the Ministry of Human Rights of Pakistan started a free nationwide helpline to report domestic abuse cases. People could report cases by calling 1099 or by using the Helpline 1099 application on a mobile device.

In some countries, new bills or national action plans addressing VAWG were adopted during the pandemic, and this may have been in part driven by the increased attention to VAWG. For instance, in 2020 Uzbekistan established a fund for the support of women and families, which involved support for rehabilitation centers whose role is to provide emergency medical, psychological, social, pedagogical, legal, and other assistance to people faced with family problems and domestic violence. Meanwhile Azerbaijan approved in November 2020 its first National Action Plan to combat domestic violence for 2020–2023.

As explained, all measures tackling VAWG are gender sensitive by definition (footnote 70). Looking at the other policy areas this tracker refers to, however, the picture is a bit less positive.

In regard to labor market measures, less than one-quarter of tracked measures are gender sensitive (Figure 9). Labor market measures include legislation on wage subsidies and income replacement for the self-employed, labor regulatory adjustments for the labor market, activation measures, as well as reduced work time and telework policy (Table 5).

### Table 5: Types of COVID-19 Policy Measures Tracked and Implemented in Central and West Asian Countries

| Economic, Financial, and Fiscal Support for Businesses And Entrepreneurs |
|---|
| Credit lines or additional liquidity by financial institutions |
| Credit/loan deferral, restructuring or renegotiation |
| Equity injections: public sector loans to businesses |
| Equity injections: public sector subsidies to businesses |
| Loan guarantees |
| Multiple measures |
| Tax cut, exemptions, credits |
| Tax deferrals |
| **Labor Market** |
| Activation measures and enterprise development |
| Labor regulatory adjustment |
| Reduced work time and telework |
| Wage subsidy and income replacement for self-employed |
| **Social Protection** |
| Social assistance |
| Social insurance |
| **Violence Against Women** |
| Awareness raising campaigns |
| Collection and use of data |
| Integration of VAWG in COVID-19 response plans |
| Other measures |
| Strengthening of services |

COVID-19 = coronavirus disease, VAWG = violence against women and girls.
Source: United Nations Development Programme. COVID-19 Global Gender Response Tracker Database (accessed March 2022).

Among the labor market measures in CWA that were considered gender sensitive, the COVID-19 Solidarity Fund in Kazakhstan, a labor activation measure that also targeted women in its skills development training programs. Gender-sensitive wage subsidy and income replacement measures were also implemented in the region, e.g., through one-off payments to medical workers infected with COVID-19 and one-off payments to families of medical workers who died due to COVID-19 infection in the Kyrgyz Republic, where women represent around 83% of the health care workers. On the other hand, an example of a labor market activation measure that was not classified as gender sensitive was the Kamyab Jawan Program in Pakistan, which readjusted its technical training of youth in conventional and high-tech trades to virtual training and e-learning, with no specific focus on how to guarantee access by female youth.

In terms of social protection, only 14% of measures were classified as gender sensitive. Social protection policy includes social assistance measures like cash transfers, social pensions, utility or housing support, and social insurance measures, such as parental leave, unemployment benefits, paid sick leave, or pensions.

Among the gender-sensitive social assistance measures implemented in Armenia and Georgia were cash transfers to pregnant women (support package No. 7 in Armenia), cash for care of unemployed parents (support package No. 9 in Armenia) and in-kind support for vulnerable families in Georgia, including women-headed households, single parents, ethnic minorities, LGBTQI community members, Roma settlements, and other vulnerable groups. Relevant public bodies, such as the Office of the State Minister of Georgia for Reconciliation and Civic Equality, the Tbilisi Mayor's Office, local municipalities, and the Prime Minister's Human Rights Council, participated actively in the process of organizing and distributing the in-kind support.

An example of a gender-sensitive social insurance measure was found in Uzbekistan, where childcare paid leave was granted to a working parent (only one of the two) for the duration of schools and kindergartens being shut down without affecting the regular annual paid leave schedule of the parent.

Some social insurance measures, such as unemployment benefits in Azerbaijan, were gender-neutral, as they did not differentiate between men and women. Mandatory health insurance introduced in Azerbaijan in 2021 with universal coverage of the population was a gender-neutral measure.

About half of economic, financial, and fiscal support for businesses and entrepreneurs were classified as gender sensitive, better than for other policy areas. These were considered gender sensitive if they provided support to female-dominated sectors of the economy. In Uzbekistan, a measure providing tax deferrals and interest-free loans for the payment of wages to SMEs in the tourism sector was considered gender sensitive, because the tourism sector employs 1.6 times more women than men. Tax deferrals and equity injections through public sector loans to businesses benefiting sectors where women's MSMEs are concentrated were also put in place in other CWA countries including Armenia, Georgia, Kazakhstan, and the Kyrgyz Republic. Gender-blind fiscal measures benefiting the private sector included liquidity injections into commercial banks, such as in Georgia.

## What Has ADB Done? ADB's COVID-19 Response in Central and West Asia

Some measures put in place by governments in CWA were financed through grants or loans provided by multilateral development banks, which were at the forefront of the COVID-19 pandemic crisis response for countries with limited domestic fiscal capacity. ADB in particular has been praised for moving rapidly to provide a range of instruments supporting its developing member countries (DMCs).[69] But were ADB's COVID-response initiatives gender sensitive? What lessons and opportunities can we learn from them?

---

[69]    R. Aboneaaj et al. 2022. Multilateral Development Banks' Crisis Response: What Instruments Do MDBs Offer and How Fast Do They Act?. *Centre for Global Development Note*. 14 March.

The comprehensive and diverse package of loans and grants that constituted ADB's COVID-19 response in CWA was meant to support governments to contain and tackle COVID-19 impacts from different angles. The package was reviewed in June 2021 by the Independent Evaluation Department, which recognized several major achievements: notably, that ADB responded quickly and effectively to the pandemic and prepared and committed operations at an unprecedented scale. Support was mainly channeled from mid-2020 through the COVID-19 Pandemic Response Option (CPRO), an expenditure support program, as well as via emergency assistance loans (EALs) and emergency assistance grants (EAGs). Special assistance grants (SAGs) were also provided in 2020, while the Asia Pacific Vaccine Access Facility (APVAX) launched in 2021. In total, 23 projects of these four typologies were approved In CWA in 2020 and 2021, worth a total of $3.64 billion (Figure 10).

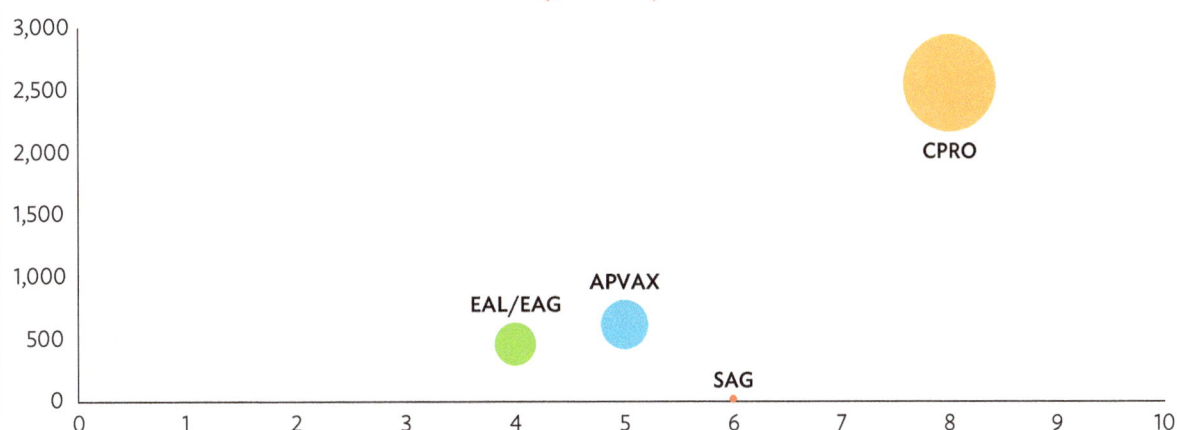

**Figure 10: Number (axis x) and Value (axis y) of COVID-19 Response Initiative Projects by Type of Initiative in Central and West Asia, 2020–2021**
($ million)

APVAX = Asia Pacific Vaccine Access Facility, COVID-19 = coronavirus disease, CPRO = COVID-19 Pandemic Response Option, EAL = emergency assistance loan, EAG = emergency assistance grant, SAG = special assistance grant.
Source: Author's computation based on the Asian Development Bank projects database.

The greatest share of these interventions, both in terms of monetary value and number of projects, was CPRO projects: eight projects worth $2.55 billion. EAL and grant projects also represented a significant amount of ADB's COVID-19 response in CWA, accounting for three loans and one grant for a total of $480 million. The APVAX facility covers five CWA countries and cost $615 million. SAGs were provided through the Asia Pacific Disaster Response Fund with the support of the Government of Japan for a total of $15 million in six countries. According to ADB's gender classification of projects, all of the CPRO, EAL, EAG, and APVAX initiatives were classified as effective gender mainstreaming (EGM), so they all included either a gender monitoring matrix (GMM) or a gender action plan (GAP).[70]

---

[70] All sovereign and nonsovereign ADB projects are assigned one of four gender mainstreaming categories: Category I: gender equity theme; Category II: EGM; Category III: some gender elements; and category IV: no gender elements; ADB. 2021. *Guidelines for Gender Mainstreaming Categories of ADB Projects*. Manila.

The country accounting for both the highest number and highest value of projects is Pakistan (Figure 11). Kazakhstan received the second highest contribution to its COVID-19 response from ADB in the region, totaling over $1 billion, followed by Uzbekistan ($603 million), and Azerbaijan ($250 million). Some projects were cofinanced by other multilateral development banks like the Asian Infrastructure Investment Bank (e.g., in Uzbekistan) and the World Bank (e.g., in Pakistan), as well as recipient governments.

**Figure 11: Number (axis x) and Value (axis y) of COVID-19 Response Initiative Projects in Central and West Asia, by Country, 2020–2021**
($ million)

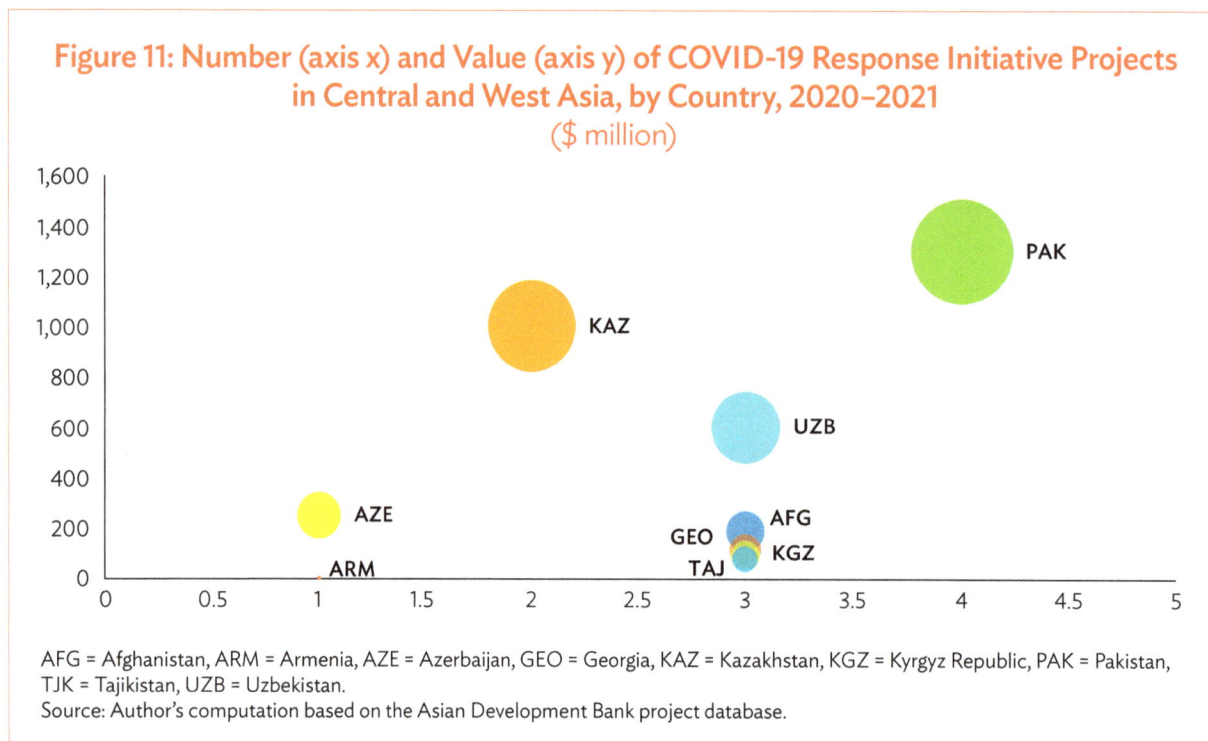

AFG = Afghanistan, ARM = Armenia, AZE = Azerbaijan, GEO = Georgia, KAZ = Kazakhstan, KGZ = Kyrgyz Republic, PAK = Pakistan, TJK = Tajikistan, UZB = Uzbekistan.
Source: Author's computation based on the Asian Development Bank project database.

## CPRO: Emerging Evidence on Lessons and Opportunities to Improve Gender Responsiveness

The CPRO was established under the Countercyclical Support Facility and designed as a tool to facilitate critically needed fiscal stimulus for developing member countries to better manage the immediate economic and financial shocks created by the pandemic. It was created by modifying the conditions under the existing Countercyclical Support Facility and represents a variation on conventional policy-based lending. However, unlike conventional policy-based lending, which requires fulfilment of policy actions prior to disbursement, CPROs only require evidence of eligibility, as measured by six access criteria. This made it possible for the ADB to quickly disburse fiscal support to governments in need.[71]

---

[71]   A. Sato et al. 2021. How Effectively is the Asian Development Bank Responding to COVID-19? An Early Assessment. *Centre for Global Development Policy Paper*. No. 226. August.

Requests for CPRO support were spread broadly across ADB country groupings and regions. The Southeast Asia Department accounted for almost half of all committed CPRO support by commitment amount, followed by the CWA Department at about 23%. On a project count basis, CWA processed the most CPRO operations compared with other ADB subregions.

Eight CPROs were financed in CWA, five of which have been closed (Figure 12).[72] They all have similar structures and focus on a few main outputs, including strengthening the health system and COVID-19 response, improving social protection for the most vulnerable (including women), and support to the private sector, business, and employment. In lower-middle income countries like the Kyrgyz Republic and Tajikistan, at least part of the funds was in the form of grants and they included measures aimed at guaranteeing food security.

## Figure 12: COVID-19 Pandemic Response Option Initiatives in Central and West Asia, by Country, 2020–2021
### ($ million)

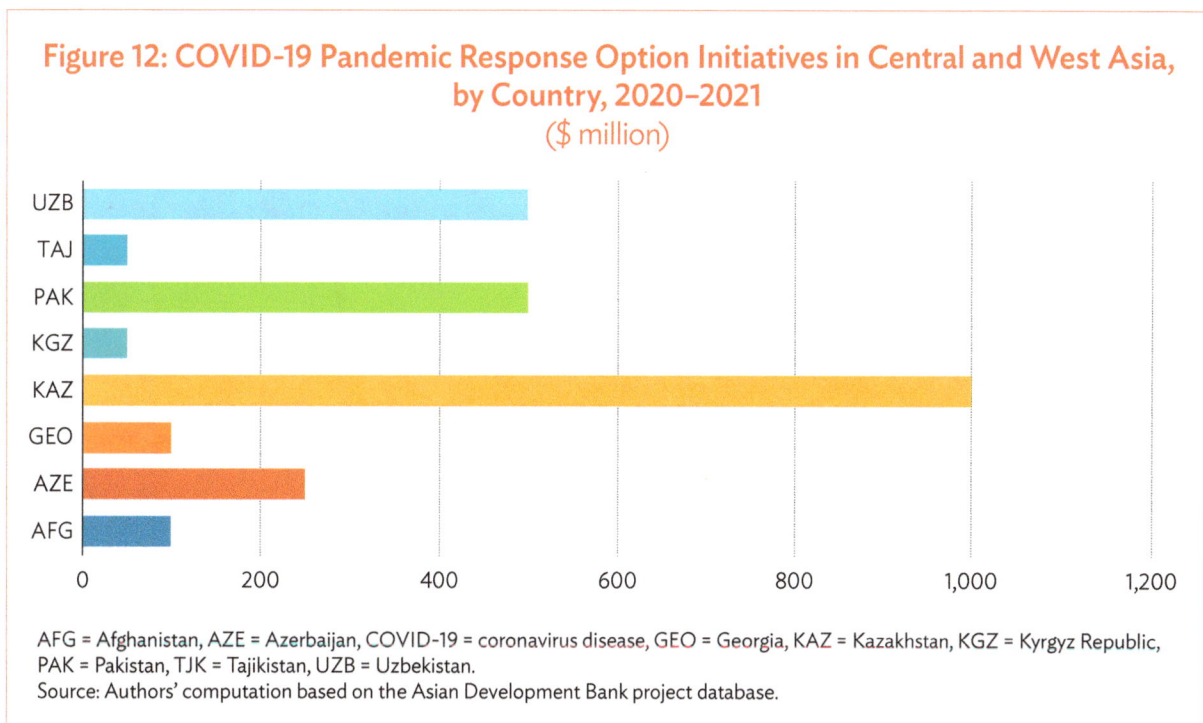

AFG = Afghanistan, AZE = Azerbaijan, COVID-19 = coronavirus disease, GEO = Georgia, KAZ = Kazakhstan, KGZ = Kyrgyz Republic, PAK = Pakistan, TJK = Tajikistan, UZB = Uzbekistan.
Source: Authors' computation based on the Asian Development Bank project database.

An internal review of CPROs highlighted that they are efficient and appropriate instruments for responding to ADB developing member countries' needs, commending the record level of financing achieved.[73]

From a gender perspective, emerging evidence shows that ADB's efforts to mainstream gender and development considerations into its COVID-19 support has been successful. The inclusion of an effective, pro-poor countercyclical expenditure program as access criteria for CPRO support increased the focus of operations on the social assistance, economic stimulus, and health measures to be taken to address COVID-19-related impacts. This expanded financing for social protection and vulnerable groups, including women and girls. The requirement to assess the criteria, together

---

[72] Two CPROs were still active as of March 2022, one in Azerbaijan and one in Kazakhstan. ADB placed its regular assistance on hold in Afghanistan effective 15 August 2021.
[73] ADB. 2020. *ADB's Comprehensive Response to the COVID-19 Pandemic: Policy Paper*. Manila.

with GMMs, enabled ADB to engage in meaningful dialogue with government counterparts, tailoring approaches that made the best use of ADB's resources to mitigate the impacts of the pandemic, with an emphasis placed on poor and disadvantaged groups, including women and girls and the most vulnerable populations (footnote 75).

This was also confirmed by the review of the Kyrgyz Republic and Tajikistan CPROs that was carried out in the framework of this assessment. Project completion reports for these two initiatives had already been developed at the time of writing, showing they were successful in terms of relevance, effectiveness, and efficiency, as well as gender equity. In both countries, the support provided through CPROs helped the government to address the social, health, and economic impacts of the COVID-19 pandemic through a government-led program that was coherent, highly relevant, efficient, and delivered at unprecedented speed. In addition, many of the performance indicators had specific gender targets, which helped these governments to deliver on their commitments to women's empowerment at a time when women were disproportionately affected by the impacts of the pandemic. Some general features of the Tajikistan CPRO are presented in Box 3.

### Box 3: Tajikistan's COVID-19 Pandemic Response Options

**COVID-19 Active Response and Expenditure Support Program – $50 million**

**Outputs**
- Health measures for COVID-19 country preparedness and response implemented.
- Increased social assistance and food security measures implemented.
- Enhanced support for business entities and measures to safeguard employment implemented.

ADB rated this program successful in terms of its relevance, effectiveness, and efficiency, as well as in terms of gender equity.

**Key gender-related achievements include:**

- The program directly benefited female health care workers by ensuring that all health workers, regardless of gender, directly working with COVID-19 patients were properly protected with an adequate quantity and quality of properly fitting personal protective equipment and by providing female health workers with menstrual hygiene kits as needed. About 40,000 medical workers (including 29,600 female workers) received personal protective equipment and menstrual hygiene kits. These items were distributed to medical workers in 41 health facilities throughout Tajikistan. This measure met the specific needs of female health care staff and helped avoid higher exposure and infection risk among female doctors and nurses. In addition, separate female and male COVID-19 wards and facilities for medical workers were created. The program also enabled a salary supplement equivalent to 100% of the current monthly salary of frontline medical workers (81.5% of whom are women) directly managing COVID-19 cases.

- A significant number of women and girls in poor households were recipients of the Targeted Social Assistance program. The program reached 115,744 households headed by women (51.7%), of which 67,600 (41.6%) were headed by women with children younger than 3 years old.

- The number of beneficiaries who received one-time social assistance of TJS500 (about $45) in 2020 was also significant. Of the 64,469 households that received this assistance, 36,876 (57.2%) were headed by women.

- The program also provided temporary tax relief and other financial support (concessional lending) to crisis-affected micro, small, and medium-sized enterprises, including those owned by women, to help them recover. This helped to mitigate income loss for women entrepreneurs and business owners and maintain employment. According to the gender monitoring matrix and business registration statistics, tax concessions benefited about 30,175 business entities, while only one sixth of planned concessional lending was actually disbursed, which was short of the performance indicator.

ADB = Asian Development Bank, COVID-19 = coronavirus disease.
Source: Author.

The analysis of GMMs, which are used to monitor gendered achievements, showed that in general, good quality monitoring mechanisms were prepared for all CPROs.[74] However, some technical aspects could be improved and qualitative indicators could be included in order to improve the quality of the matrixes and the depth of findings on the effectiveness and gender responsiveness of these programs.[75]

For some measures, the assumption is that since women are targeted, they are benefiting appropriately. Targeting women in the percentage that they are represented in the reference population, as is done with health workers and female-headed households, is necessary but may not be enough to spur gender transformative change, which implies that existing gendered power imbalances are corrected. It should be noted however that this was a deliberate strategy for the CPROs due to their emergency nature, the logic being to ensure equitable access to projects' resources and not leave women behind. In any case, improved gender indicators could be useful particularly for social protection outputs/program.[76]

This finding is closely related to the need to collect and disseminate more sex-disaggregated data to improve monitoring and gender responsiveness of policies. This includes statistics produced by administrative data, as this is often the source for many monitoring indicators of public investment initiatives. In Tajikistan for example, the government has not been able to collect sex-disaggregated data in some instances. It has been noted that the CPRO design could have focused more on building the capacities of developing member countries to develop gender-disaggregated data rather than requesting such inadequately collected data during an emergency. The inclusion of data collection targets within the GMM should help monitor gender achievements and develop evidence-based recommendations for future interventions.

Some general recommendations that stem specifically from the analysis of the Kyrgyz Republic and Tajikistan CPRO project completion reports have important gender implications. They mostly reflect priorities for policy options and public investment identified by stakeholders in key informant interviews (Section 7).

## Emergency Assistance Loans, Asia Pacific Vaccination Facility, and Special Assistance Grants: An Overview

Four emergency assistance loans and grants were approved in CWA countries in 2020 totaling $460 million (Figure 13). They are still ongoing as of March 2022 and are classified EGM. Two implemented in the Kyrgyz Republic and Uzbekistan are mainly focused on strengthening the health system. The EAG in Afghanistan also focused on the health sector (footnote 20). The EAL in Pakistan on the other hand contributes to the same outputs as the CPRO, i.e., it contributes to social protection channeled through the Benazir Income Support Program, Pakistan's social protection agency.

---

[74] Preparing a GMM is one of the requirements of projects classified as EGM.

[75] In the results framework of some CPROs, e.g., the Kyrgyz Republic and Tajikistan, indicators at the outcome level were not specified properly, which impacted also on GMM quality. In other CPROs, specified indicators are unlikely to be measurable due to unavailability of data. For Pakistan, for instance, there are doubts as to whether the gender indicators specified are appropriate to monitor the program due to a lack of availability of data.

[76] For conditional cash transfer programs, for example, many studies have been conducted on the way different conditions may or may not constitute an additional burden for women involved, hence some qualitative indicators might be useful to improve the understanding of the gendered impact of these policies.

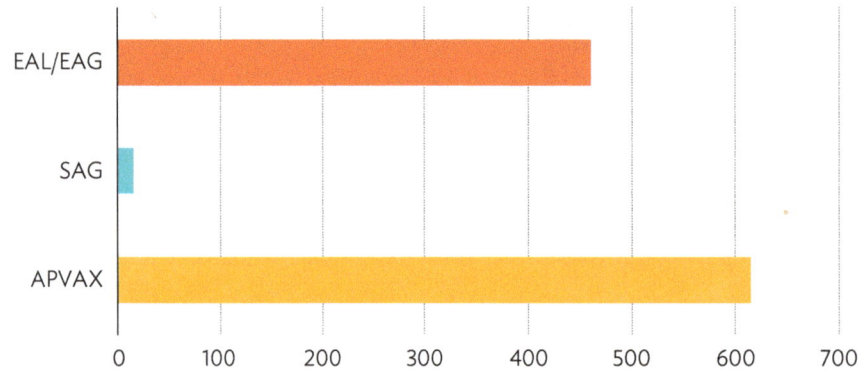

**Figure 13: Emergency Assistance Loans, Asia Pacific Vaccine Access Facility, and Special Assistance Grants Initiatives in Central and West Asia, 2020–2021**
($ million)

APVAX = Asia Pacific Vaccine Access Facility, EAL = emergency assistance loan, EAG = emergency assistance grant, SAG = special assistance grant.
Source: Authors' computations based on the Asian Development Bank project database.

From a gender perspective, all the EAL projects are EGM, i.e., most outputs have a gender performance indicator, and therefore GAPs and gender indicators to track progress have been specified. An in-depth review is still not possible as these programs are ongoing as of March 2022; however the review of their GAPs pointed at the need to strengthen the use of qualitative gender targets as well as quantitative ones. The initial review also commends the inclusion of the gender-responsive activities specified in the GAPs, such as providing all health workers with timely access to COVID-19 testing and setting up and making operational a monitoring system on COVID-19 with sex- and age-disaggregated data. Another gender responsive action is the expansion of COVID-19 treatment capacity, which includes hardship allowances and incentives for health workers, who are mostly women. The Uzbekistan EAL is described in Box 4.

### Box 4: Uzbekistan's Emergency Assistance Loan

In Uzbekistan, the value of the emergency assistance loan is $200 million, of which $100 million was provided by ADB and $100 million cofinanced by the Asian Infrastructure Investment Bank. The aim is to increase the efficiency, quality, and accessibility of health care while containing transmission of COVID-19. The project's outcome is to reinforce the resilience of the health system to outbreaks of COVID-19 and other public health emergencies, through three outputs: a strengthened national laboratory system, a national surveillance and response system established for COVID-19 and expansion of COVID-19 treatment capacity.

ADB = Asian Development Bank, COVID-19 = coronavirus disease.
Source: ADB. 2020. Report and Recommendation of the President to the Board of Directors. Proposed Loan and Administration of Loan. Republic of Uzbekistan. *COVID-19 Emergency Response Project*.

In 2021, the APVAX initiative was launched and loans were provided to promote vaccination in Afghanistan, Georgia, the Kyrgyz Republic, Pakistan, and Tajikistan (footnote 20). The highest APVAX loan in CWA as of March 2022, $500 million, was to Pakistan, also the most populous country in the region. The smallest APVAX loan, $15 million, was granted to Georgia. These projects all aim at reducing the spread, morbidity, and mortality of COVID-19, particularly for vulnerable groups, while restoring the confidence of citizens and following national vaccination development plans. They all have the same two outputs (Box 5).

## Box 5: Asia Pacific Vaccine Access Facility in Georgia

The Asia Pacific Vaccine Access Facility project in Georgia has two outputs: COVID-19 vaccine procured and delivered to designated points, and vaccine program implementation capacity strengthened. Gender-responsive activities specified in the Gender Action Plan include the development and implementation of a sex-disaggregated monitoring system, conducting a satisfaction survey among vaccine recipients on vaccine services received; building capacity of health workers on globally accepted protocols on gender-sensitive and safe vaccination practices, and a review of the extent of gender responsiveness of current guidelines and communication plans on vaccine administration.

Georgia has suffered from one of the highest rates of spread of COVID-19 in the world and the implementation of this project aimed at reducing significantly the mortality of men and women from COVID-19 in a gender-responsive manner.

COVID-19 - coronavirus disease.
Source: ADB. 2021. COVID-19 Vaccine Support under the Asia Pacific Vaccine Access Facility: Gender Action Plan. Manila.

ADB's support complements other development partners' assistance to support vaccine procurement and delivery and strengthen program implementation capacity, including the World Bank, the European Investment Bank, UNICEF, and WHO. ADB is in regular consultation with development partners through the United Nations resident coordinator and on a bilateral basis. Since these projects have just recently begun implementation, there are no evaluations yet. However, from a gender perspective, it can be noted that all the APVAX projects are EGM, which means that GAPs and gender indicators to track progress have been specified and national gender specialists have been hired, at least in some countries.

Six SAGs were also provided though the Asia Pacific Disaster Response Fund with the support of the Government of Japan, for a total of $15 million. These grants were aimed to provide countries with logistics support and complement other initiatives. They included the improvement of laboratory diagnostic and testing capacity, and procurement of personal protective equipment and other medical equipment to help the government meet its most urgent needs.

# Chapter 7

# Policy Options and Priority Actions for a Gender-Responsive COVID-19 Recovery in Central and West Asia

## Priority Area 1: Economic Security

Priorities may change somewhat among countries, with some prioritizing women's entrepreneurship and others highlighting the importance of regulation and labor rights, but the main priority action that was identified by stakeholders in all countries is improving economic security and access to income-generating opportunities for women.

## Strengthen Gender-Responsive Employment Policies and Social Protection

Most countries in CWA underlined the need to strengthen social protection systems and reduce the vulnerability of women who are informal or seasonal workers.[77] Interviewees suggested strengthening and extending social protection to uncovered groups (e.g., informal workers) but also to design and implement social transfers in gender-responsive ways. This was particularly stressed in countries like Pakistan, Tajikistan, and Uzbekistan, though the need to maintain or strengthen measures around income support for workers and households was highlighted in all countries. In Uzbekistan, for example, a governmental stakeholder highlighted the need to accelerate the adoption of a law on social insurance that is currently being developed. The same stakeholder also recommended increased integration of policies in the areas of poverty reduction, social protection, and employment.

In regard to the policy area of labor market institutions and rights at work, many CWA countries, but especially South Caucasus ones, highlighted the need to eliminate discriminatory practices toward women in the workplace. These practices include prioritizing men over women for career advancement, and may be related to pregnancy and/or maternity, or to other disparities that hinge on women's traditional care role. It should be noted that some of these practices may be legal or in a gray area, so regulation should encourage a cultural change. Stakeholders across the region called for fairer and broader coverage of labor market institutions including minimum wages and employment protection, as well as improved protection of women from violence and harassment at work. As a governmental stakeholder in Uzbekistan emphasized, it is also necessary to further regulate remote working, with special attention to work-life balance. Even though some regulation for public workers already exists, the need to develop policy in this area was stressed.

---

[77] The actions and policy priorities specified by stakeholders in key informant interviews were analyzed and reorganized using as a reference the integrated gender-responsive employment policy framework to support gender-responsive recovery, presented in: ILO and UN Women. 2021. *Assessing the Gendered Employment Impacts of COVID-19 and Supporting a Gender-Responsive Recovery. A Country-Level Policy Tool*. Geneva.

Skills development has also been identified as a priority area in most CWA countries. Stakeholders in Azerbaijan, Georgia, Pakistan, and Tajikistan all emphasized the need to reshape skills development in line with post-COVID labor demand and ensure equal participation of women and men in new fields. Skills development measures that were identified by stakeholders in the region, particularly in Tajikistan, include reducing digital gender gaps, and encouraging and supporting women and girls' education and training in science, technology, engineering, and mathematics fields. This should also contribute to "taking concrete measures to reduce the role of women in the shadow economy," as an Azerbaijan civil society representative also noted.

In general, all measures aiming at improving equal opportunities for women in the labor market should contribute to reducing informal work, though specific policies to engage women in the formal sector are also needed. As an informant pointed out, in the Kyrgyz Republic, they are trying to increase the proportion of female formal workers versus female informal workers. However, to do this, it must be beneficial for workers to "come out of the shadows," as one informant phrased it. Governmental actors in Uzbekistan stressed the need for women to enter formal employment.

At the level of sectoral policies, most countries stressed the need to support traditionally female sectors and occupations but also identify promising sectors in line with long-term policy goals of gender equitable structural transformation. In Azerbaijan and Tajikistan, the need to extend digital infrastructure and reduce gender gaps in access was highlighted. The Kyrgyz Republic stakeholders called for the need to diversify women's employment.

Countries where agriculture is one of the main sectors of employment for women include the Kyrgyz Republic, Pakistan, and Tajikistan. In these countries, stakeholders underlined the need to pay more attention to women's terms of inclusion in agriculture. Policies related to land, agriculture extension services, and technology should be designed and implemented in gender-responsive ways. It is important also to ensure that women farmers are not left behind in efforts to promote commercial agriculture. One particular risk is that the persistently informal character of female agriculture labor can downgrade the social status of female workers by excluding them from benefits that men typically harvest. Civil society in Tajikistan underlined the importance of considering the access of women to modern affordable energy-saving equipment. They also stressed the importance of the rehabilitation of drainage and irrigation canals. In Kazakhstan, the need to attract investors to rural areas and create formal jobs for women was highlighted.

In regard to active labor market policies, using public procurement to generate employment for women in sectors where they are likely to predominate, and using public work programs to especially support poor women dependent on casual work for survival, were also recommended in line with global evidence.

Finally, even though stakeholders did not emphasize the macroeconomic level, it is worth noting that gender-responsive polices recommended by the International Labour Organization to improve women's employment in the post-COVID recovery and that are applicable to CWA countries include the following:

- In the recovery phase, avoid fiscal adjustment and sustain public spending on infrastructure that is critical for well-being to stimulate aggregate demand;
- Increase public investments and support private investment toward sectors that have strong employment potential and produce essential goods and public services for all;

- Broaden the tax base through formalization and tax wealth, addressing tax evasion and reducing the incidence of tax on poor women; and
- Provide international financial support to countries that do not have sufficient capacity.

## Promote Women's Entrepreneurship

Stakeholders belonging to various sectors of society all highlighted the need to develop and strengthen women's entrepreneurship as a top priority. The importance of the private sector and the role it can have in promoting gender equality and women's empowerment was also repeatedly emphasized.[78]

To this end, an enabling environment is essential, as was highlighted by interviewees in Pakistan and other countries. In other words, it is important to create a broad-based and mutually reinforcing policy infrastructure in support of women's entrepreneurship. This framework is partially available in some countries but was called for in others, such as Tajikistan, where CSOs highlighted that their recent efforts to get specific measures on women's entrepreneurship approved by the government have not been successful. Global evidence shows that using a dual-pronged approach to prioritize women's entrepreneurship by enacting gender specific laws and strategies, as well as mainstreaming gender concerns into broader statutes and regulations regarding MSMEs is effective (e.g., in the Philippines).[79]

The diverse set of measures to develop women's entrepreneurship that stakeholders specified in the interviews are in line with existing global evidence, which indicates that holistic interventions, combining capacity building, networking, and access to finance components are among the most effective methods to support women entrepreneurs.[80]

Stakeholders in Armenia also noted that women entrepreneurs consider access to finance as the most significant barrier to entrepreneurship, in line with the most prominent challenges faced by women entrepreneurs worldwide (footnote 36). However, financing alone may have only a minimal effect on entrepreneurial development and that financial support is most effective when offered in combination with training and mentoring. One of the main measures that was highlighted in all countries but especially in Pakistan, Tajikistan, and Uzbekistan, is the need to design and/or strengthen programs that aim at developing women's capacity to grow their businesses through integrated loan-and-training programs, while helping them to transition from microfinance to standard banking. In Uzbekistan, where centers for women's entrepreneurship have been created at the provincial level, stakeholders pointed at the need to strengthen this system and make it more effective.

Overall, initiatives that aim to increase women's access to finance and make banks more responsive to the needs and priorities of women entrepreneurs should focus on improving gender mainstreaming into the finance sector itself. International evidence shows that greater gender integration at the staff and board levels of financial institutions results in business products and services that work better for female customers. For example, women may be more likely to purchase new, innovative products or

---

[78]   Noted by stakeholders attending ADB CWA workshop in March 2022.

[79]   ADB and The Asia Foundation. 2018. *Emerging Lessons on Women's Entrepreneurship in Asia and the Pacific. Case Studies from the Asian Development Bank and The Asia Foundation.* Manila and San Francisco.

[80]   ILO. 2018. Entrepreneurship Development Interventions for Women Entrepreneurs: An Update on What Works. *Issue Brief No. 7.* Geneva.

services from another trustworthy woman, and may feel more confident asking questions about their use and maintenance (footnote 35). To better respond to the needs of female clients and employees, some banks are also working to get certifications for businesses that promote gender equality within their organization, like for example the EDGE-certification.[81]

Finally, stakeholders especially in South Caucasus countries noted the importance of information and communication technology for women's entrepreneurial development, while Pakistani observers highlighted the importance of developing women's entrepreneurship in the online business sector. Regional evidence shows that leveraging this technology to ease access to business development support services and reduce barriers to accessing finance are good practices.[82]

## Priority Area 2: Violence Against Women and Girls and Health

Improving the systems that prevent and respond to VAWG was identified as one of the pressing priorities for post-COVID recovery efforts, together with women's economic security.

First of all, many stakeholders agreed that referral systems need to be improved and that multisectoral response mechanisms need to be strengthened or established to provide effective protection and prevention for victims and survivors. This appeared even more clearly during the first stages of the pandemic when response and coordination became increasingly challenging.

Stakeholders in Tajikistan and Uzbekistan all pointed to the need for improved coordination between law enforcement, judicial authorities, health care centers and crisis centers, as well as to the importance of referral systems. In Uzbekistan, civil society representatives noted that coordination, especially at the local level needs to improve. They also noted that the pandemic helped establish intersectoral interaction between the government and nongovernment organizations in the prevention of domestic violence, particularly with the justice system. Azerbaijan also underlined the importance of functioning referral systems at the national and local levels.

In regard to existing legislation and action plans or strategies to combat VAWG, the situation in CWA is quite diverse. However, in general there is a need to review existing legislation for its adequacy in effectively preventing and eliminating VAWG. Where no laws on VAWG exist, such laws urgently need to be passed and implemented. In Kazakhstan, the need to strengthen legislation has been stressed while it is seen as urgent to push the agenda that domestic violence should not be solved through informal mediation. In Azerbaijan, civil society and development partners noted that that the Istanbul Convention must be signed and that it is necessary to ensure the effective functioning of the law on domestic violence. Draft amendments to the domestic violence and criminal code were presented to the Cabinet of Ministries. In Tajikistan strengthening legislation is also called for, as well as its effective implementation. The State Program on Prevention of Violence, adopted by law, has no budget.

---

[81]  EDGE Certification is the leading global standard for diversity, equity, and inclusion, centered on a workplace gender and intersectional equity approach.

[82]  A specific brief of the ADB on how information and communication technology is essential to promote women's entrepreneurship in CWA is an important reference to further develop recommendations and design actions in this policy area: ADB. 2014. Using Information and Communication Technology to Support Women's Entrepreneurship in Central and West Asia. ADB Brief No. 23. Manila.

Many countries need to update or develop action plans. The Government of Georgia, development partners, and civil society have all recognized that important steps have been taken to fight VAWG, including from a peace and security perspective, and action plans developed with the cooperation of different actors were to be presented as of March 2022.

In regard to the delivery of services and their quality, adequate training for law-enforcement staff and health and social workers is of utmost importance to guarantee access to justice and services for victims and survivors. The need to increase the number of shelters and other protections services has been highlighted in nearly all countries. Sufficient funding that guarantees longer-term access to effective services for victims and survivors is therefore an absolute necessity.

Interviewees stressed that digital systems introduced during the pandemic should be further developed. However, one problem that came up in Armenia, Kazakhstan, and the Kyrgyz Republic is that digital or phone reporting systems that were boosted during the initial phases of the pandemic are not having the necessary continuity.

Finally, data collection on VAWG must be improved.

## Develop Preparedness Plans and Decrease Gender-Biases in the Health Sector

Public health experts are concerned delayed care caused by the pandemic could do lasting harm to the health system and patients, even after the immediate burden of the pandemic eases.

In general, the main recommendations that stakeholders have given in regard to improving gender responsiveness of public investment in the health sector has to do with developing or improving preparedness plans, including the establishment of adequate additional allowances for medical staff who respond to crises. The need to enhance gender sensitivity of doctors and medical staff was also underlined. As an Uzbekistan governmental stakeholder put it, "We need more professionally trained specialists, because based on the population of the country and the number of families, specialists working on gender issues are a drop in the ocean. We need to work extensively in this regard."

In addition, increased attention to intersecting forms of vulnerability is needed. This includes pregnant women who need to access reproductive health services, persons with disabilities who faced barriers to access routine health care services during the pandemic, and other groups with specific health vulnerabilities.

## Priority Area 3: Unpaid Care and Domestic Work

As noted, one effect of the pandemic has been an increased recognition of the value of UCW in sustaining economies and to highlight that women disproportionately carry this burden. To achieve women's economic empowerment and inclusive growth, equal access to paid and decent work needs to be complemented by an egalitarian distribution of UCW among men and women.

Most stakeholders in CWA identified asymmetries in unpaid care and domestic work as a priority area to work on in the medium to long term, and mentioned measures that should be implemented. Given the diversity of policy frameworks, a regional one-size-fits-all solution would not be effective. However, countries can work on at least five policy areas to tackle this imbalance and enable women to enter or return to the job market.[83]

In the first place, it is essential to recognize and represent unpaid work in policies and decision-making, which implies carrying out a detailed analysis of the care economy in each country and of the gaps in available public care services for different groups. This means looking in-depth into existing services for both preschool and school-age children, along with older persons, and persons with disabilities.

In Azerbaijan, Georgia, and Tajikistan, for example, the difference between availability of care services in urban and rural areas was highlighted. In Azerbaijan public childcare facilities in rural areas are way more limited than in urban areas, where 24% of kindergartens are funded by the state. One of the first steps in designing a gender-responsive care policy is therefore to have a clear assessment.

Another area to work on to redress the unequal distribution of unpaid work within households is strengthening employment rights and workplace policies. This was particularly stressed by stakeholders in South Caucasus countries. It includes formalizing parental leave for both women and men, as well as improving awareness of the benefits of flexible work schedules and different types of working arrangements that will facilitate more equal distribution of unpaid work and that will help women and men find a better work-life balance. In Tajikistan, stakeholders stressed that legislation on parental leave and its application are not clear (see Appendix, which provides an overview of legislation on parental leave in some CWA countries).

As most stakeholders emphasized and the literature shows, the main problem underlying the disproportionate burden of unpaid work on women are social norms. In Pakistan a high-level development partner highlighted the need to "build on the current momentum and develop a strong narrative for the recognition of UCW undertaken by women. Again, the youth of this country can be involved to change their perspective and attitudes towards it." The need to challenge social and cultural norms was also underlined by governmental stakeholders in Uzbekistan, who recommended focusing on the role of gender-sensitive education and the importance of including it from early childhood. "We need good programs, we need to teach children to appreciate, respect, and value women's role in society... This must be taught from childhood." Tajik stakeholders also insisted that the first step to take is changing the worldview that a woman should be first of all a good bride and a housewife.

Investing and prioritizing social care infrastructure is another priority action mentioned by many stakeholders in the region. This includes support to ensure accessible and affordable child and older persons care and public services to reduce women's unpaid work responsibilities and to enable their labor force participation.[84] As stakeholders in most countries, but especially in Armenia, Azerbaijan, Georgia, and Tajikistan, noted the link between the UCW burden and access to economic opportunities is evident. These measures are therefore clearly connected to the effectiveness of

---

[83]    United Nations Economic Commission for Europe and UN Women. 2021. *Empowering Women through Reducing Unpaid Work: A Regional Analysis for Europe and Central Asia.* Geneva.

[84]    UNDP. 2021. Investing in Care: A Pathway to Gender-Responsive COVID-19 Recovery. New York.

employment and entrepreneurship policies described earlier. Gender-responsive budgeting initiatives at the macroeconomic and local levels can help to ensure that resources are allocated to such public investment.

Finally, improving the legal and institutional infrastructure of social protection systems is also essential. This includes strengthening social assistance and social insurance programs and schemes to ensure that they enable a decent standard of living. Measures aiming at universalizing pension entitlements and other social allowances, rather than basing them on working life and earned salaries, were also highlighted. These were among the measures most cited by informants, as in the wake of the pandemic most unpaid caregivers, at least in some countries, could not benefit from social allowances. Stakeholders stressed repeatedly that to decrease vulnerability of women, who are often informal workers or just poor, some social protection policies that guarantee survival are necessary.

It is therefore essential to develop social protection programs that support unpaid caregivers and that avoid penalizing women for this role. These and other recommendations should be taken in consideration when designing and expanding social protection programs. For example, the Benazir Income Support Program in Pakistan and the programs that are being implemented under its umbrella could benefit from a reflection on the opportunity of unconditional cash transfer systems that weaken gender stereotypes and that avoid creating additional care-related burdens for women. In the Kyrgyz Republic, the need to expand existing innovative measures of social care was also stressed.

## Priority Area 4: Decision-Making, Public Finance Management, and Data Collection

At least three action areas came up clearly relating to decision-making and women's leadership. Valuable recommendations were identified based on stakeholder interviews.

First, improved cooperation between governments and civil society and development partners was called for. Especially in South Caucasus countries, but also in Tajikistan, CSOs have called for an increased and more meaningful cooperation with governments. Women's participation in social protection policymaking is particularly important to promote, ensuring dialogue and consultations with women's groups and CSOs. Moreover, in Azerbaijan specifically, a change in the nongovernment organization law was demanded as it is seen as significantly limiting the public role of civil society, including in the promotion of women's rights.

The need for increased gender expertise and capacities within governments was also noted by CSOs and development partners in the region; governments themselves partially recognized the need to improve their gender expertise. This is particularly the case for social protection and labor policies, as noted by several key informants. Measures here include capacity development to analyze laws and policies from a gender perspective, gender statistics, and public procurement.

The lack of gender strategies and gender equality laws was also underlined in some countries, such as Pakistan, while in countries where institutional and legal frameworks for gender equality exist, improved implementation and intra-governmental coordination was called for.

Civil society, especially in Armenia and Azerbaijan, underlined the need to develop preparedness plans, explaining that the pandemic was a "wake-up call." An Armenian women's activist pointed out that, "No one can guarantee that we will not face such incidents again. The government needs to know the sequence of actions in the event of an emergency and must clearly identify vulnerable groups."

Finally, most CWA countries have gender-responsive budgeting in place or have piloted initiatives. Georgia has a particularly rich experience in this regard, including a new public finance management system created in partnership with the Public Expenditure and Financial Accountability Program that is being currently implemented, as a government representative pointed out. Some development partners however noted that in most countries in the region the effectiveness and sustainability of gender-responsive budgeting initiatives has been limited and have called for a renewed effort to strengthen them.

Gender data collection and statistical systems capacity of governments need to be strengthened because the collection and use of timely, quality gender data by all data sources is critical to identify and tackle gender inequalities. More and better data is needed to identify to formulate gender-responsive and evidence-based policies and promote an equitable recovery.[85] Various statistics institutes in the region highlighted this need for better gender data. For example, in Uzbekistan, a strategy for improving statistics was adopted in 2020 and includes a dedicated article on gender statistics. However, development partners in Uzbekistan stressed the need for a complete assessment of the capacities of the statistical system to collect relevant gender data.

As a stakeholder in Armenia noted, new emergencies are likely to happen and it is important to be prepared, even in regard to data collection. Efforts should be taken to address methodological issues and to develop capacities in research structures and in different layers of the statistical system for good quality data collection. They underlined the specific need for reliable statistics on VAWG in Armenia, shared by VAWG experts in most countries. There is an urgent need to improve VAWG data collection systems so that they include all forms of violence and disaggregate data by age, sex, area (urban and rural), and relationship between the perpetrator and victim and/or survivor. Azerbaijani governmental stakeholders also underlined the need to strengthen methodologies.

Comparable and recent gender data with an adequate granularity however needs to be developed in most sectors. This is a crosscutting issue and it has been emphasized repeatedly by many stakeholders throughout the region and in this report. The review of ADB's COVID-19 response and existing assessments also point to this as a priority. Increased coordination on data collection and research as well as improved statistical capacities are also needed, as development partners especially noted.

---

[85]    ILO, UN Women, and World Bank. 2021. *Strengthening Gender Measures and Data in the COVID-19 Era: An Urgent Need for Change.* Geneva.

# Appendix

## Table A.1: Number of Key Informants Interviewed in Stakeholder Survey by Country and Sector

| Country | Civil Society | Development Partner | Government | Total |
|---|---|---|---|---|
| Armenia | 4 | 4 | 5 | 13 |
| Azerbaijan | 4 | 4 | 4 | 12 |
| Georgia | 4 | 2 | 6 | 12 |
| Kazakhstan | 4 | | 4 | 8 |
| Kyrgyz Republic | 5 | 5 | 3 | 13 |
| Pakistan | 4 | 2 | 1 | 7 |
| Tajikistan | 4 | 4 | 5 | 13 |
| Uzbekistan | 2 | 4 | 5 | 11 |
| **Total** | **31** | **25** | **33** | **89** |

Note: The names of respondents and interviewees are not identified in the report for confidentiality.

## Table A.2: Paternity and Parental Leave in Selected Central and West Asian Countries

| Country | Duration of Paternity Leave | Amount of Paternity Leave: Cash Benefits | Duration of Parental Leave | Cash Benefits of Parental Leave |
|---|---|---|---|---|
| **Armenia** | 146 weeks | AMD18,000 monthly (approximately $37.50) | Mothers: 156 weeks | Mothers: 104 weeks paid leave, 52 weeks unpaid. Fathers: 94 weeks paid leave, 52 weeks unpaid. The monthly cash benefit for working parents is fixed, not based on salary. |
| **Azerbaijan** | 2 weeks | $37.50 monthly for 104 weeks | Mothers only: 18 weeks | 34.5% of annual salary. |
| **Georgia** | n/a | n/a | 104 weeks, of which 26 weeks are remunerated. (28 weeks if parents have twins or if there are birth complications) | Public-sector employees: 100% salary for 26 weeks, plus GEL1,000 (approximately $390) allowance allocated by the government. Private-sector employees: GEL1,000 from the government; private-sector employers may determine the amount of salary reimbursement. |

*continued on next page*

Table A.2 *continued*

| Country | Duration of Paternity Leave | Amount of Paternity Leave: Cash Benefits | Duration of Parental Leave | Cash Benefits of Parental Leave |
|---|---|---|---|---|
| **Kazakhstan** | n/a | n/a | Mothers only: 18 weeks (10 before birth; 8 after birth). Up to 10 weeks after birth in the event of birth complications or twins Either parent: 52 weeks | Both working and not working parents can receive social benefits for a child under 1 year at a fixed amount allocated monthly. For a working parent the monthly allocation cannot exceed a T97.836 (approximately $294.50), which is equal to 40% of the minimum wage times 10. It cannot be lower than the unemployment benefit. |
| **Kyrgyz Republic** | The labor code does not specifically mention paternity leave. Its duration is determined in agreement with the employer. | SOM700 (approximately $10) are assigned in one instalment to fathers or anyone else taking on the custody role when the mother is missing. | 10 weeks before birth and 18 weeks after birth (20 to 25.7 weeks if birth complications or twins). An employer can allow additional unpaid leave to care for a child up to 3 years of age. The leave can be provided at any time for any period, but only to working women (not men). | For working parents: First 10 days – 100% of salary. From the 11th day on – SOM1,000 (approximately $14.30) from government budget. Officially registered unemployed parents: SOM1,000 from the government budget. Unemployed parents who are not officially registered are not eligible for cash benefits. |
| **Tajikistan** | n/a | n/a | Mothers only: 20 weeks – 100% paid 25.7 weeks in the event of birth complications or twins – 100% paid When maternity leave ends, women can get childcare leave until the child is 1.5 or 3 years old (benefits will differ based on child's age). | Government subsidizes child nutrition with a TJS44 ($5) monthly allowance. |
| **Uzbekistan** | n/a | n/a | | Childcare allowance is only paid to single parent or low-income families, as well as to families with children with disabilities, until a child is 2 years old. The childcare allowance is SUM299,550 ($37), equal to 200% of the minimum wage. |

n/a = not applicable.
Note: Paternity leave is a type of leave that can be taken by fathers right after the birth of a child. It is often a short period of time. Parental leave can be taken by mothers and fathers or guardians until a predefined age of the child. It is supplementary to maternity or paternity leave.
Source: United Nations Economic Commission for Europe and UN Women. 2021. *Empowering Women through Reducing Unpaid Work: A Regional Analysis of Europe and Central Asia*. Istanbul.